Winning
The Inner Game
Of
Selling

Matt Oechsli

Dedication

This book is dedicated to you—the professional salesperson with the courage to unlock your true potential.

Table of Contents

Foreword

Selling is an art form, not a science. You can learn 99 approach strategies, 266 answers to objections, 44 different closes—and still not be able to sell enough to put a decent meal on the table. Why? True greatness comes from within. Look at any superior salesperson and you will see an individual who is quietly self-confident, comfortable with himself or herself, and at peace with both business and personal relationships.

Matt Oechsli combines two rare talents. He has reached that state of self-knowledge and confidence that is a prerequisite for success, and he can teach you how to get there, too.

This book will not be easy to read. As a matter of fact, it will probably make you downright uncomfortable. I hope so.

RAYMOND E. WERNER

Introduction

The chapters that follow are specifically designed to take you through each stage of an achievement group series that I conduct in five sessions over a 120-day period. You will find my entire focus is centered around combining personal and professional growth. In other words, winning the inner game of selling requires balanced living.

I have been working with salespeople for the past 15 years. During this time I have witnessed many miraculous success stories. Unfortunately, I have also seen some very capable people fail. The successful salespeople all have one very important factor in common—they are committed to personal growth with the same enthusiasm that they apply to selling.

By simply following the techniques, principles, and tactics exactly as they are presented in *Winning The Inner Game Of Selling*, you will:

- Create magic through a working partnership;
- Master the art of Role Model Power;
- Design your life map;
- Re-record, and control, your tapes—your voices;
- Create success habits; personal and professional;
- Boost your inner confidence and self-esteem;
- Turn your dreams into a mental compulsion;
- Develop high achievement self-discipline;
- Master the power of your mind;
- Act upon your fears;

- Make your own self-programming cassette tapes;
- Turn negative stress into sales;
- Double your income if you desire to.

Every success in life, big or small, originates from within. Napoleon created battle plans from daydreams in a sandbox. Albert Einstein was an uneducated 16 year old when he imagined himself riding on a beam of light as it traveled thru space at 186,000 miles per second. An infant imagines himself walking long before he takes that first step.

Successful salespeople know they are going to achieve greatness well in advance of their achievements. High achievers are able to clearly visualize their success years before it happens. They are able to see themselves making the sales, winning the contests, living the lifestyle of their choice, and enjoying all the pride and respect that comes with success.

This visualization is the internal program of the high achiever. It encompasses an unshakable self-expectancy, a prerequisite for success in selling. It is this visualization, these internal tapes, that continually refuel your enthusiasm. These pre-programmed tapes also provide the resilience to maintain your motivation on the heels of rejection. You will learn to act, consistently, day after day.

Sounds exciting, doesn't it? Keep reading, you are starting a success journey of your own!

Chapter 1

RULES OF THE INNER GAME

Throughout this text I will refer to individual cases and companies I have worked with. Because of some of the delicate information I'll be sharing, I have changed all the names to protect the confidentiality of my clients. Everything else is straight from my files.

"I can't figure it out . . . I understand this business, inside and out, but I'm just not doing what I know I need to do. Why?" said a frustrated Chuck Adel, as he nervously fidgeted in my office.

"I'm 52 years old," he continued, "I've got an MBA, and was a national sales manager for a Fortune 50 company for 12 years. I switched careers at 42 and went into high-commission sales. I've done okay, but haven't been able to consistently make the kind of money I anticipated when I left the corporate world. My life has been a roller coaster in sales. Two years ago I was in the top five in our company, this year my production has been down in the bottom half."

As with many frustrated people, Chuck wanted to talk, so I listened as he continued, "I've lost confidence in myself. I spin my wheels with nonproductive busy work and I can't seem to get on track. The worst part is watching rookies come into the business and, without a fraction of my knowledge, out-produce me."

What caused Chuck, in the midst of success two years ago, to be struggling to stay on his feet only one year later? Why was his entire selling career slowly draining away his confidence and enthusiasm? Maybe you can relate to Chuck's dilemma. Many salespeople can.

1

Your Personal Tapes

You are where you are, today, because of the tapes that you have playing inside your head. You are who you are for the same reason—the tapes playing inside your head. Chuck Adel's selling career was being wasted because of these tapes.

What is so interesting about our vast and powerful inner dimension, is that most people are aware that it exists, and need only a little guidance to begin to understand it. After only a few minutes of talking, Chuck identified the cause of his recent slump and, ultimately, the root cause of his troubled career.

"It's funny," he said, "but when I was being recognized as a high producer at our national convention last year, I wasn't really happy. I was scared. I had doubts about the upcoming year. I can vividly remember thinking to myself that it would be impossible for me to have another great year. This thought made me extremely nervous."

Chuck had just articulated the reason for his slump, his internal tapes were self-defeating. "As I heard my name called out," he went on, "and my accomplishments recited, I felt a sinking pressure come over me. Even as I listened to the applause, a voice inside of me kept saying, 'You'll never be able to do this again next year . . . you're going to fail.' "

Well, Chuck's thoughts certainly predicted his future. We all have little voices in our heads that we listen to. The problem is that all too often these voices are extremely limiting. And believe me, they do not have to be as extreme as Chuck's to interfere with your selling career.

I refer to these internal voices as tapes because they play automatically, and they play whatever is recorded. Just like a pre-recorded cassette tape you listen to in your car, tapes play whatever is recorded every time they are played. There are only two options available; re-record the tapes, or don't listen to them.

Salespeople beware

Salespeople beware, these internal tapes have been the ruin of many promising careers. Alas, most people, not just salespeople, have the wrong recordings in their head. The messages they hear are too frequently self-limiting. Their tapes are constantly playing those devilish littles voices of doubt: "You can't do this . . . " "You'll never amount to anything in sales." "They're not going to buy from you." On and on they go—this pattern of thinking becomes a habit. It could sabotage your involvement with this book.

Please understand there is no miracle cure, but there are definite laws of nature. As it states so clearly in the Bible, "As a man thinketh in his heart, so is he." I am taking you on a natural journey.

Understanding the competition

Everybody is searching for that competitive edge, scheming to gain a distinct advantage over "the competition." Accept the fact that "the competition" is you. You have no outside competition! Your only competition is determined by the limits you set for yourself. Salespeople are habitually looking over their shoulders at their counterpart across town, when they need to be focusing attention on how well they are playing the inner game of selling.

All winners fully understand that winning is an inside game. They realize that their own accomplishments define their self-esteem, discipline, and achievement drive. The guy across town has his own battles to fight.

Winners are very cognizant that their tapes, those little internal voices, are the most critical part of their professional and personal lives. This is why you will rarely find successful salespeople spending much time with average producers. It's not arrogance; they simply guard themselves very carefully against negative influences. Average producers tend to complain a lot. Right? They are a negative influence. How about you?

Salespeople are unprepared

Unfortunately, salespeople are taught only how to play the outside game of selling. Their time and energy is devoted to worrying about the competition, digesting volumes of product knowledge, and memorizing manipulative selling techniques.

The inner game of selling is mentioned only in passing, "You need PMA (Positive Mental Attitude) to sell." "You must be enthusiastic to sell." "You've got to believe . . . . " But salespeople are left to their own resources in acquiring these critical success components—the inner game.

Why? Because most sale managers and trainers not only lack the understanding to teach the necessary skills, but are frequently listening to self-limiting tapes themselves. They habitually focus on their negatives, and of course, your negatives. They worry. They suffer from low self-esteem. So, they do the best they know how and mention the standard positive attitude cliches as they hit the street selling.

Since most managers are ill equipped to teach these inner game concepts, they remain only as abstract cliches.

While I agree with what these cliches stand for, nobody will ever change a lifetime of recorded tapes through casual reference. Telling salespeople to have positive mental attitudes, when all their lives they've been beaten down with negatives—and their tapes are playing those devilish voices of doubt—is like telling children to relax in the midst of a spine-tingling ghost story. It becomes even more difficult, if you are also scared of ghosts. Either way, the message does not compute.

Am I talking about you?

Don't be alarmed if you sense I might be talking about you. Most people are ill prepared by their parents and teachers for high achievement. Although they meant well, you were probably programmed by your primary role models, parents and teachers, to be less than a complete success. Instead of constantly reminding you how precious and capable you were, you were probably reminded of every mistake you made, everything you ever did wrong, every bad grade in school. This has a major impact on those little voices you hear.

Let's take a closer look and see if I'm really talking about you. The following Achievement Drive Profile is a simple tool to help gauge your current preparation for achievement. You will find the basis of my work revolves around Socrates' famous dictum, "Know thy self!"

Make certain you complete every profile as it appears. I have situated them strategically throughout the book. At times, there might appear to be some redundancy. This is only normal, as every part of our personal and professional lives, our mind, body and soul, are inextricably linked.

The good news is that you can change. You really can become the successful, complete person you always dreamed of becoming. Imagine yourself with more confidence and enthusiasm than you ever experienced in your life. See yourself totally focused, full of positive energy, actually enjoying every minute of every working day. Visualize yourself with perfect harmony at home, with a loving, caring, supportive family.

Does this sound too good to be true? For those of you with those little devilish voices, I'm sure it does. But this is no idle daydream, it's not a rah-rah pep talk. Through the power of your own mind, I am going to teach you step by step how to take control by re-programming your subconscious mind (those tapes), and ultimately win the inner game of selling!

4

ADP: Achievement Drive Profile

Instructions: This exercise is designed to help you measure your current preparation for achievement. Your responses to various past situations will facilitate a better awareness of the real you. For best results, answer each question as honestly as you can now. You are measuring how you are today—not as you would like to be. Circle the number under the answer that best describes you.

	Strongly Agree	Mildly Agree	Mildly Disagree	Strongly Disagree
1. At times I feel frustrated and question myself.	4	3	2	1
2. I tend to blame others for my shortcomings.	4	3	2	1
3. I don't like salespeople.	4	3	2	1
4. I lack persistency and have trouble completing what I start.	4	3	2	1
5. I find myself getting sidetracked more easily than I like.	4	3	2	1
6. I keep a close account of the hours I work.	4	3	2	1
7. I feel as though there is tremendous pressure to perform.	4	3	2	1
8. I tend to dwell on my mistakes.	4	3	2	1
9. I struggle with rejection and take it personally.	4	3	2	1
10. I am constantly working to improve my skills by reading books, listening to tapes, and attending seminars.	1	2	3	4

Scoring the ADP: You will determine your ADP score by adding the numbers circled.

Maximum Score = 40   My Score _____

Score

40 — 36	You better invest a minimum of two hours a day to the exercises in this book. Your lack of achievement drive is holding you back BIG TIME!
35 — 29	You will be able to get your achievement drive working with work—make it a top priority!
28 — 21	Average. Your mild achievement drive is holding you back in the manner of most salespeople.
20 — 14	Your achievement drive is strong and ready to become a valuable asset!
13 —	Please write me after you've completed this book! The sky's the limit!

Areas For Improvement:

Review the individual items on the Profile and determine specific areas that you need to develop, strengthen, and enhance in your efforts to eliminate procrastination and improve performance. If you:

Circled **4**, you've identified an area to **develop.**

Circled **3**, you've identified an area to **strengthen.**

Circled **2**, you've identified an area to **enhance.**

Select *three areas* to work on between now and your next group meeting. List them below and discuss them with your partner.

#1— _____

#2— _____

#3— _____

What Is the Meaning of Life?

Winning The Inner Game Of Selling is about life. There are no "puppy dog" closes to learn, no magic telephone presentations to memorize, and no dress codes to follow. Rather, you will be learning how to make magic from what you already know. My observation, from working with thousands of salespeople, is that most know too much of the outer sales game, like Chuck Adel, and produce too little.

Action Step: In a moment I'm going to ask you to stop reading, close your eyes, and imagine yourself as the high achiever you want to be, full of confidence and positive energy. I want you to imagine all the details; the clothes you would be wearing, the jewelry, the car you would drive . . . Okay, close your eyes and spend 90 seconds imagining.

How did that feel? Could you see the images associated with your achievement? Granted, some people can imagine more easily than others, but everyone is capable with practice. As simple as that little "controlled daydream," that image you created is the foundation of *Winning The Inner Game Of Selling!*

Wrap-Up

- You are *where* you are because of the tapes inside your head.
- You are *who* you are because of these same tapes.
- Your internal tapes play whatever is recorded.
- Chuck Adel had all the knowledge but was hostage to his tapes.
- Your only competition is deep down inside of you.
- You can change your tapes, your internal programming.
- There are no miracle cures, rather definite laws of nature that will lead you to success.
- What is the meaning of your life?

IMPORTANT STUFF!

1. List below the stuff you found important in this chapter.

    _____

    _____

2. What do you want to change? _____

    _____

    _____

3. When are you going to change it? _____

    _____

    _____

4. What are you going to enhance?_____

    _____

    _____

5. How are you going to enhance it? _____

    _____

    _____

Chapter 2

YOUR WORKING PARTNER

Are you prepared to embark on a journey that is going to touch every part of your life? Are you ready for an adventure that is going to place complete responsibility for all of your accomplishments—personal and professional—on you? And, would you like to substantially increase your income in the process?

If the answer is yes, the chapters that follow will show you how. Although I will serve as your teacher, guide and master mentor, it will be up to you to do the changing.

Your mission, then, is to maximize your potential as a human being. As I've already mentioned, no lasting change can occur without balance in your life. For this reason, I must insist that you be prepared to develop a lifestyle for a lifetime. Each exercise, every action step, every chapter is designed to take you step by step to the successful completion of this mission. This is your journey of self-mastery—your Mission Possible!

So, as the Nike® advertisements state so succinctly, let's "Just Do It!"

The Magic of Sharing

You will find me using the word "magic" in describing various components of the inner game because they are so simple and can make an immediate impact. Sharing your inner growth will bring out this kind of power.

Whenever I conduct a program, I always ask the participants to share within 24 to 48 hours what they've learned. The reason is simple, the value of information is enhanced when the student assumes the role of the teacher.

The effect of this is tremendous. People take better notes, pay closer attention, get more involved because now they are planning to teach this material to someone else. It can be a spouse, a significant other, a colleague . . . it doesn't really matter. What is important is that action is created.

Unfortunately, this is not as powerful when you are learning from a book. It simply takes too long for most people to finish reading an entire book. Still, remember about the magic of sharing. Because of the nature of book learning, I've decided to suggest a proactive alternative.

A working partnership

Even in my live programs, I don't stop at asking people to teach what they learn. Like any homework assignment, I know many people with the best intentions will never get around to teaching. For this reason, I require proactive involvement with peers. This is designed to be carried on indefinitely into the future by all participants.

What I'm asking for is a buddy system approach to personal and professional growth. You need to start thinking about teaming up with a peer. This person will be your working partner.

Support groups—one day at a time

People all over the world are discovering that by concentrating on what they can control, and through talking, listening, and sharing with their peers, long-term change can be accomplished. The power of a working partner relationship is well illustrated by the success of the AA.

Dr. Robert Smith and a New York stockbroker named Bill Wilson developed an historic working partnership that evolved into the founding of Alcoholics Anonymous. No breakthrough discoveries were made on the causes and cures of alcoholism, just like no breakthrough developments have occurred in professional selling. What Smith and Wilson discovered was that there was something magical about peers, fellow sufferers, supporting each other.

Eventually Bill Wilson refined his working partnership concept into a program that is now the foundation of most support groups; the famous "twelve steps."

Regardless of the endeavor, be it sales, school, relationships, family, or overcoming alcoholism, in order to get results you've got to pay your dues! Managing prioritized specific activities is paying your dues. The catch is, there is no such thing as a free lunch, you've always got to pay.

Your commitment to your daily activities is much like the motto of AA, "one day at a time." You can handle that. Your working partner will assist you with feedback, support and accountability, but only you can do it.

Choosing your working partner

Start by considering the professional salespeople who you seem to connect with. An individual who shares similar aspirations, sales experience, and earnings. Basically, the working partnership needs one person teamed with another who is approximately at the same level. The magic is lost if you team up with your boss. Your working partnership requires a peer who will read this book, get involved with the exercises, and grow!

This you can do! You can find another salesperson who is willing to help you, to help himself or herself.

Please be careful in selecting a partner in your journey for success. You must team up with an individual who shares a similar desire to dream, act and grow. If not, your partner will pull you down. The person will try to steal your dream of mastering the inner game of selling, because the individual has never really had one of his or her own.

But, a well-chosen working partnership will develop into a synergy between peers. Rather than looking at your counterpart as competition, you will each become an active member of the other's success team.

You will schedule a weekly meeting of your success team where various growth exercises are discussed, experiences are shared, feedback is given and received, and both players hold each other accountable to keep pace with their success journey.

Be assured that the idea of peers supporting peers is not a new concept in the world of business and achievement. Back in 1876, a scientist with less than three months of formal education formed what he called a Master Mind Alliance. The intent was to pool the talents of engineers, model makers, scientists, mathematicians and skilled mechanics. Sixty-one men in all, intent on helping each other grow. They planned for a minor invention every 10 days and a major invention every six months. In less than six years, the uneducated founder of this group, Thomas Edison, had more than 300 patents! Peers supporting peers is timeless.

11

Please note: To make true magic out of this book you need to read it, discuss it, and complete all the exercises with a peer. Each of you should purchase your own copy, establish regular reading assignments and meetings. You will share and accelerate your growth.

A working partner is priceless!

Feedback * Accountability * Support

The objective of your working partnership is to develop a bond with another salesperson that transcends competitive jealousies. You are essentially putting into action the old phrase, "The more you help someone else achieve their goals, the closer you come to realizing your goals."

Establish the number of chapters you're both going to read for the upcoming week, and agree to work through all the exercises. When you meet, start off by discussing the chapters. Then share any exercises that require completing. When you get to the chapters requiring a commitment to specific fixed behaviors, this is where accountability becomes extremely important.

What you will soon realize through your working partnership is that you're both more similar than dissimilar. You have similar fears, anxieties, challenges, dreams and aspirations. But now you no longer have to do it alone. You are no longer the Lone Ranger—you have support!

Let me define what I mean by feedback, support and accountability.

Feedback: To be effective, feedback must be helpful, constructive, and call for a specific action. It cannot be criticism! It must also be welcome by the receiver. There can be no defensive posture. Discussion is to follow only after the feedback is given.

Support. Genuine interest and concern for the successes and challenges facing your working partner is a must. Nothing happens when one person is too self-serving. This must be a true "win-win."

Accountability. The objective of your working partnership is personal and professional growth. Each partner must allow the other to hold the individual accountable for the growth they feel is important. This is not just a feel-good rap session. If your partner hasn't completed the exercises, make it understood that you will not accept that behavior. We all need a little nudge, and we must be willing to accept it. You must allow yourself to be held accountable by your partner. This is targeted peer pressure!

FASP: Feedback Accountability Support Profile

Instructions: This short profile will assist you in differentiating between criticism and feedback, love and support, accountability and rationalization. You need to be fully aware of your past tendencies. For best results, answer each question honestly.

	Strongly Agree	Mildly Agree	Mildly Disagree	Strongly Disagree
1. I tend to get defensive when someone questions my actions.	4	3	2	1
2. I resent people giving me advice.	4	3	2	1
3. I get uncomfortable listening to others speak earnestly about their goals.	4	3	2	1
4. I am reluctant to share my inner self with others.	4	3	2	1
5. I rationalize my daily activities, regardless of my initial daily plan.	4	3	2	1
6. I can be highly critical of others.	4	3	2	1
7. My spouse is terrific as he, she, supports everything I do.	1	2	3	4

Maximum Score = 28   My Score _____

Score

28 — 21   You need to pay close attention to all working partner exercises. Relax, this is new to most.

20 — 14   You have some feel for true feedback, *accountability* and support. Now it's time for daily application!

13 — 11   Without realizing it, you already are benefiting from your peers.

10 —   You're great! Keep it going.

Areas For Improvement:

Review the individual items on the Profile and determine specific areas that you need to develop, strengthen, and enhance in your efforts to eliminate procrastination and improve performance. If you:

Circled **4,** you've identified an area to **develop.**

Circled **3,** you've identified an area to **strengthen.**

Circled **2,** you've identified an area to **enhance.**

Select *three areas* to work on between now and your next group meeting. List them below and discuss them with your partner.

#1— _____

#2— _____

#3— _____

Your personal needs analysis

As you begin your search for a working partner, it's a good idea to identify your strengths and weaknesses. In what areas do you excel? What do you perceive as barriers to unlocking your human potential? What has been holding you back?

The following list is simply a guide. Feel free to expand on it as you like.

Strengths	Weaknesses
Attitude	
Enthusiasm	
Achievement Drive	
Discipline	
Persistence	
Knowledge	

Communication
Health
Energy
Family
Loyalty
Integrity
Humor
Appearance
Creativity
Courage
Empathy
Work Ethic

I am accountable to correct: _____

I accept feedback to compensate for: _____

I welcome support and accountability to capitalize on:_____

YOUR WORKING PARTNERSHIP AGREEMENT

Signature _____   Date _____

Signature _____   Date _____

This document is very important to your personal growth. Keep it where you can refer to it regularly and update it at your weekly partnership meetings. As soon as you establish a working partnership, go over this agreement together. Often your partner might have some insight to your strengths that you might have overlooked. Most people seem to be well versed in their weaknesses.

So many simple inner game tactics are overlooked. For instance, there has been little or no emphasis placed on role models. Yet any student of human behavior will attest that personal development is tremendously enhanced by a positive, human example. The most rapid growth in children occurs when they still naturally identify parents as role models. This is why your parents, and subsequently teachers, played such a pivotal role in creating your personal tapes. Not all parents and teachers served as positive role models.

Are you a positive role model? The following chapter will not only show you how to find a role model, but also, how to become a role model.

You have just begun your journey towards being the best you can be. Find a working partner, read on, and go for it!

Wrap-up

- You will dramatically accelerate your growth with a working partner.
- A working partner is a person who shares your desire to grow personally and professionally.
- Feedback, support and accountability are critical components of a working partnership.
- Know your strengths and weaknesses.

IMPORTANT STUFF!

1. List below the stuff you found important in this chapter.

_____

_____

2. What do you want to change? _____

_____

_____

3. When are you going to change it? _____

_____

_____

4. What are you going to enhance?_____

_____

_____

5. How are you going to enhance it? _____

_____

_____

Chapter 3

DOUBLE YOUR INCOME

If you were able to consistently perform up to your potential for the next 12 months, would your income double? Some salespeople can do more. Others are in Chuck Adel's position—just looking to maintain—but most can double their income by winning the inner game.

Therefore, I begin this chapter with an income challenge to the working partnership; double your income over the next 12 months. Commit to it.

I like to put monetary objectives in front of salespeople because it astounds them when they realize, as you will too, that income will be substantially increased as they improve all the other facets of their lives. This means that your personal life and family will not suffer for your success—quite the opposite will occur.

Why, you might ask.

Self-Image Psychology

The great Maxwell Maltz first legitimized the concept of self-image psychology. His two classics, *Psychocybernetics*, and *The Magic Power of Self-Image Psychology*, were built on his conviction that human behavior is determined by the self-image held within each individual.

Even though this concept is no longer new, most people have spent little, if any, time *developing* their self-image. In fact, most people have no idea of the limitations they have set for themselves by accepting a poor self-image as an unchangeable condition.

This is often very evident with overweight people. Regardless of the number of attempts some people make at losing weight, even those with the strongest willpower end up failing. Not because they couldn't lose weight, but because they could not see themselves as healthy and fit persons who enjoy their natural weights.

I've worked with many people, helping them win the inner game of natural weight control. One of the first requests I make is that they take a picture of a healthy and fit person, Christie Brinkley or whomever, cut the head out of the picture and replace it with theirs. This, coupled with their mission to become healthy and fit, works at helping change the self-image. In a matter of weeks, people who have suffered for years because of obesity, can actually see themselves as that picture. And, when they do, they start to become that picture. Only after the self-image is changed, can they truly create a lifestyle for a lifetime centered around health and fitness.

Your self-image

What is your self-image? Can you see yourself as infinitely successful? What was your emotional response when I challenged you to double your income? If you could already visualize yourself there, living all the benefits of your accomplishments, your self-image is ready for you to achieve. It will assist you in every way.

However, if you're like many of the salespeople I've worked with, just the thought of doubling your income creates tension. Part of you senses what a positive effect the additional finances will have on your life, while the other part does not believe that you can accomplish such a feat.

Examine this feeling. Learn to recognize it. Whenever this feeling occurs, it is telling you that your self-image needs some positive attention.

We all think in terms of images. If I say the numbers 1, 2, 3, what does your mind do? It sees the images of the numbers just as they are numerically presented in the preceding sentence. Your mind does not spell out the number o-n-e, and so on. We think in images at all times.

Those old messages, recorded on tapes in your mind, have created your self-image. Throughout this book I will be involving you in exercises that concentrate on changing the thoughts you program into your subconscious mind, and the subsequent self-images you create. This will create that synergistic power that is necessary for lasting significant growth.

Self-image exercise revisited

In a moment I will again ask you to stop reading, close your eyes and visualize your success. This time I want you to see yourself receiving a paycheck that is twice what it would normally be . . . picture yourself dressed in the clothes that you associate with this level of income . . . see yourself getting into your new car. Try to sense as much detail as possible; jewelry, colors, feelings, sounds.

Okay, close your eyes and visualize this self-image.

How did you feel? This is an excellent exercise to practice with your working partner. Share your images. If you had trouble getting those images in your mind, did you recognize the feeling? Thoughts that interfere with this exercise are a reflection of the specific behaviors that are holding you back. For instance, many salespeople have thoughts of prospecting—they imagine the telephone, or a cold call—dominating their success self-image. This is because their subconscious is signaling that call reluctance has been holding them back.

Is call reluctance the real problem? No, it's only a symptom. The real problem is deep inside; it's the self-image.

Working partner exercise:

Discuss the images you were able to visualize. Determine how naturally, or unnaturally, these success images were able to stay in your mind. Share with each other the thoughts, if any, that interfered with your success images. Was there any tension? Did you enjoy the exercise? Discuss your thoughts about the power of self-image.

Imagination Power

In a moment, I will again be asking you to close your eyes and visualize. But, this time your self-image will not conflict with the picture. Your physical well being might be at stake, but your self-image won't be threatened.

Picture yourself on a balcony on the twenty-seventh floor of a high rise apartment building. There is no guard rail on the balcony. You're sitting in a chair, safe in the middle of the balcony, but two little children are playing on the balcony, sometimes getting dangerously close to the edge. They sit to play right near the edge and you have to walk over to them and get them inside. You're fully aware of the 27-floor drop and no guard rail. Okay, close your eyes and visualize this scene.

21

Wow! I got a little queasy just writing this! How did you feel? Most people feel almost as if they were there. The same people whose self-image interfered with pictures of success, can easily create these alternative images. Even though they are discomforting, and the images centered around potential physical harm, there was no conflict with the self-image.

There are two very powerful insights to be considered from these two exercises. First, the phenomenal power that your self-image holds on your life, your accomplishments, your potential. Second, how easily the subconscious mind can interpret false images as real. There was no balcony without a rail on the twenty-seventh floor, yet, because the subconscious can be fooled, you react as if the event were real.

I will get into much greater detail about the conscious and subconscious mind later in the book. But for now, keep in mind that many of the challenges I will ask you to accept will be in contrast to both your internal tapes, and your self-image. But all of this will soon change.

The 21-day action plan

Your mission is a 21-day action plan that will enable you to begin changing the tapes in your head. You will be mastering your greatest sales tool—your mind! I am going to teach you how this powerful sales tool works. As you learn the art of feedback, support and accountability with your working partner, success habits will seem to evolve as your self-image improves. This growth always occurs in tandem.

You're going to have fun with the exercises; you're going to enjoy growing and bonding with your partner. The more you practice, the more second nature control of your inner power will become.

A Monetary Perspective

Indulge yourself for a few moments about thoughts of money. What changes will take place in your life when you double your income? How will you feel about yourself? How will your friends and co-workers react towards you? How are you going to handle the change?

I am always asking salespeople the following question, "Why live to make a living, when you can live to make a life?" Why be in bondage to a job because of a lack of resources, when you can be free? I want your imagination to begin conjuring up images of financial freedom. Since I have an advantage of knowing how the mind works, I'm going to continually repeat certain messages that I want programmed in your subconscious.

Such as, financial freedom!

Money is really only a medium for exchange. Gold, silver, spices, horses and livestock have been used by different cultures as a medium of exchange. Now we use plastic.

Regardless of the medium, the timeless universal truth is that money is a reward for labor. The more superior the achievements, the more substantial the rewards.

Your income challenge

Discuss with your partner the prospects for your upcoming year. What could you possibly earn? How much more efficient would you need to be? After this discussion you both must make two basic commitments:

1. I commit to be the *best* I can possibly be in every area of my life.

2. I am willing to *pay the price* to be the best.

Now after you have both agreed to your basic intention of commitment, I want to establish the ground rules; *if you are not prepared to earn a lot of money in professional sales, get out of the profession.* There are many other honorable professions that will offer a moderate income, without the pressure, rejections, and damage to self-esteem. But, before you get out of selling, finish reading this book with your partner. You might be pleasantly surprised.

Average performance lowers self-esteem

It has been my observation from working with salespeople that average performance damages self-esteem. Even though the income from this average performance is well above the norm for our society, the mere fact that other salespeople earn more hurts.

A vicious cycle frequently develops. When self-esteem is damaged, a person feels vulnerable. This vulnerability impairs the achievement drive as a means of protection against any more hurt. The hurt so many salespeople end up protecting against is rejection. We all know that nobody likes being rejected. But in the sales game, it's a fact of life! The more successful the salesperson, the more rejections the individual has heard.

When a salesperson starts to lose confidence, rejection is taken personally, production drops, excuses are invented, and personal development begins moving in reverse. This is a deadly cycle! Without a healthy regard for yourself, and your abilities, you cannot sell. Self-esteem is as critical to your performance as your performance is to your confidence in your abilities.

Have you ever encountered this career-damaging cycle? Many salespeople struggle through their entire life so fully engulfed in this self-defeating cycle that it adversely affects every area of their lives.

Poverty is a mental disease

Your life will never be the same again. Poverty really is a mental disease. Every time you allow your self-esteem to be damaged, you become a little poorer inside. As a salesperson confronts internal poverty, low self-esteem and confidence usually become a major concern. Financial poverty soon follows.

Winning the inner game of selling provides you with the tools to control your self-esteem, understand the power of achievement, the reward value of money, and the magic of creating a balanced life. As you prepare yourself, with your working partner, for your lifelong journey of personal and professional growth, *make a commitment to wealth.*

I remember clearly the saga of an enthusiastic young life insurance agent, four years in the business, working for a company that I was consulting with. "I have a real problem with your attitude about making money," Jack whispered to me during a break in one of my in-house seminars. "There are many more important concerns in the world than the money I make."

Jack was correct. The world is often unfair. There is war, starvation, environmental concern, inadequate education, drugs . . . to name just a few problems that are facing the human race. However, Jack was masking a more serious internal challenge, because if he really felt that strongly about certain causes, he would be doing something about it. This came to a head in a private meeting following the seminar.

Jack became visibly hostile when I expressed my doubt concerning the validity of his reasoning. "Who are you trying to fool?" I asked, and followed up with, "How has your production growth been throughout your four years as a life insurance agent?"

"My first year was my best," Jack replied argumentatively. "I almost made rookie of the year, but then other things became more important. I proved to myself I could make it in this business, and other aspects of life became more important. I resent your income challenge."

The sad part about Jack was his honesty crisis. He wouldn't allow himself to be true to himself. I later went over his production with him and the numbers were abysmal. He was barely making enough money to pay rent on a small apartment and pay the loan on his car.

A couple of weeks later, Jack left the company. His manager said they had been trying to get him to leave for over a year, but were too kind hearted to ask for his contract. Did Jack take a job with the Peace Corps or some urban ministry? No! He became a new recruit for another insurance company on the other side of town. Poor Jack will continue to damage his self-esteem, as long as he stays in the sales game without making a commitment to wealth.

Salespeople earn more millions than doctors

There are no real secrets to winning the inner game. There are no secrets to success. *U.S. News and World Report,* in their January 13, 1986 issue, reported a study conducted on one million millionaires. What caught my attention was that most had been working for 20 to 30 years, had eaten meat and potatoes, were frugal, and were more likely to be a salesperson than a doctor. A salesperson! Wow!

Year after year I'm continually amazed, as I travel the country working with salespeople, that the majority can easily double their incomes—if they desire. All they need is a little inner game guidance. In 1988, my firm conducted a needs analysis with 1700 salespeople, which indicated that close to 90 percent of the salespeople surveyed could double their prospecting efforts. And, one company I was working with had conducted their own study. They determined that a mere 20 percent increase in prospecting activity would translate into a doubled income for their salespeople.

Add the figures for yourself.

Ask your working partner about his prospecting. Can he double his efforts? How about you? How would your business grow if you were to double the number of prospecting calls you make in a day?

Before you get involved with making your income decision, it's imperative to know whether your self-image is going to support or sabotage your efforts. As I've mentioned, you will never conduct yourself consistently in a manner that is inconsistent with your self-image. Yet, many salespeople go through their entire careers without actively addressing the situation. Ego interference prevails as they never admit a weakness in self-image. This is also why most never come close to realizing their potential.

The following profile is going to focus on the real inner you. You might feel tempted to circle responses as you would like them to be, or as you pretend them to be. *Don't!* Now is the time to be brutally honest with yourself. Your achievements will grow in proportion to honesty coupled with effort. As William Shakespeare wrote, "This above all: to thine own self be true."

SIP: Self-Image Profile

	Strongly Agree	Mildly Agree	Mildly Disagree	Strongly Disagree
1. At times I wish I were somebody else.	4	3	2	1
2. I don't trust my judgment and get opinions from others on most decisions.	4	3	2	1
3. I wish I had taken time to get more education.	4	3	2	1
4. When I think of success I'm flooded with thoughts of failure.	4	3	2	1
5. Deep inside I question my capability and confidence.	4	3	2	1
6. At social or business events, I feel like I don't fit in.	4	3	2	1
7. Sometimes I don't like myself.	4	3	2	1
8. I am my own toughest critic.	4	3	2	1
9. I have trouble visualizing my future successes.	4	3	2	1
10. It is hard for me to be open and honest with people.	4	3	2	1
11. I am not careful about the foods I eat.	4	3	2	1
12. I seldom exercise.	4	3	2	1
13. I tend to compare myself with others.	4	3	2	1
14. I feel other people get lucky breaks, but never me.	4	3	2	1
15. Deep inside I feel I am worthy of success.	1	2	3	4

Maximum Score = 60   My Score _____

Score

60 — 54   Your self-image is your major obstacle! Commit to changing it with the exercises in this book and eliminate your sabotaging behavior.

53 — 43   Your self-image is poor and holds you back more than you realize.

42 — 30   Average. But average isn't good enough for high achievement.

29 — 22   Your self-image has helped you achieve in the past. Use it consistently and you will amaze yourself!

21 —   Go for everything you can!

Areas For Improvement:

Review the individual items on the Profile and determine specific areas that you need to develop, strengthen, and enhance in your efforts to eliminate procrastination and improve performance. If you:

Circled **4,** you've identified an area to **develop.**

Circled **3,** you've identified an area to **strengthen.**

Circled **2,** you've identified an area to **enhance.**

Select *three areas* to work on between now and your next group meeting. List them below and discuss them with your partner.

#1— _____

#2— _____

#3— _____

Working Partner Exercise:

Get together with your working partner and make your income decision now! In a few months, you will be able to use your spouse as a contributor to this process. But for now, it's best to keep family out of this decision for a couple of reasons. First, as much as they will love the additional income, they don't see you as that kind of provider and might mock your ambition. Secondly, there is a tendency to mistakenly equate increased income with increased working hours, at the expense of the family. You will prove both of these concerns to be wrong.

Circle the figure that best represents the extra money you are going to earn this year. Consider this to be "plus" money because it's beyond what you are currently earning. You are not in competition with anyone else, especially your working partner. Your function is to support each other.

Remember, think in terms of doubling your income.

$25,000	+ +
$50,000	+ +
$100,000	+ +
(write your own)	+ +

Whatever figure you choose, make it a working partner commitment. Decide how much prospecting activity you must generate daily to have a good chance of reaching your figure. This will create tension, and all tension seeks resolution. Your resolution will be mastering the content of this book as you grow with your partner.

As a professional salesperson, your income decision, the plus money figure you decided on, is the reason for winning the inner game of selling. Stick with your income decision, and move on to mastering the remaining components of the inner game of selling.

Now that you and your working partner have established a specific income figure for the next 12 months, you have created a tangible reason to grow, as well as provided yourself with a system of measurement. You can keep score, and most salespeople love to keep score.

With this in mind, you are well positioned to enjoy the maximum benefits of *Winning The Inner Game Of Selling*. You have just completed a major sale—to yourself!

In the next chapter I will share with you a simple, and powerful, process that has been used by successful people for thousands of years.

You will learn how to identify heroes, recognize their strengths and weaknesses, and model specific qualities of strength as you direct them into your life.

Get ready to grow through "Role Model Empowerment." Your journey into the inner game has just begun!

Wrap-Up

- You have the right to wealth.
- You will always perform in harmony with your self-image.
- You can change your self-image, but first you must be aware of it.
- You must make a commitment to your working partner.
- Make your income decision with your partner.
- Determine your daily prospecting activity that supports your income decision.
- Allow your working partner to hold you accountable to both your income decision and prospecting activity.
- A 1988 survey of 1700 salespeople by The Oechsli Institute concluded that close to 90 percent could double their prospecting.
- Determine to be the best you can be.
- Agree to pay the price to be the best.
- Money is a reward for good labor.
- Financial freedom is yours for the taking!
- Your working partner is your support system.
- Always allow for feedback, support and accountability.

IMPORTANT STUFF!

1. List below the stuff you found important in this chapter.

_____

_____

2. What do you want to change? _____

_____

_____

3. When are you going to change it? _____

_____

_____

4. What are you going to enhance?_____

_____

_____

5. How are you going to enhance it? _____

_____

_____

Chapter 4

ROLE MODEL EMPOWERMENT

One of the more effective ways to gain an understanding of the awesome power of a role model is to study the most uninhibited phase of human learning and growth—an infant. A life form of pure energy, a tiny baby is like a fresh sponge, absorbing all the stimuli of his little world.

Naturally gathering and storing information through sight, touch, sound, movement and energy, an infant is free from the encumbrance of opinions, attitudes and self-limiting beliefs. There are no internal tapes inside this devourer of sensory input.

Often without any awareness, parents immediately take on nature's designation as a role model for their children. (This is why you share many of the mannerisms and habits of your parents.) Young children are very impressionable, and yet they are relatively free from worries, self-criticism, and the many needless fears that are so characteristic of adults.

And, it's no coincidence that most children dramatically slow their learning curve as soon as they begin to copy their parents' self-limiting habits . . . self-criticism . . . fear of failure . . . low self-esteem.

Parent Role Model Exercise

Have you ever given much thought to the habits and specific behaviors that you have acquired from your parents? Which of them have made a major impact on your life? Some of the impact has been constructive, but other acquired behaviors are questionable, if not destructive. Right?

If you're like most adults you have created a blind spot to these destructive acquired behaviors. This is a defense mechanism. It's not pleasant to think about your parents' negative behaviors, especially when there is an underlying fear that some of them might have rubbed off on you. Observe a brother or a sister. Have they inherited any of negative behaviors of your parents?

Extensive research by family therapists indicates conclusively that negative behavior is learned and passed on from generation to generation. Dr. Susan Forward in her book, *Toxic Parents*, cites numerous cases where a parent, who was verbally abused as a child, verbally abuses her own children. Dr. Forward writes of adults, beaten by a parent as child, beating their children.

I have worked with numerous individuals suffering from low self-esteem and poor self-image because of poor attitudes and habits learned from their parents. Every one of these persons could list their parents' character flaws, and they all stated that they did not want to suffer from the same afflictions.

However, role models are very powerful. For example, as these people watched their mother worry about her weight, criticize her body, and use food as a pacifier, they, in turn, worried about their weight, felt uncomfortable with their body and ate for the wrong reasons. The result? They eventually became their role model, obese. Ouch!

This power does not have to be an enemy. In fact, this is the law of the mind that you will be turning into an ally throughout this book.

Awareness is the most critical aspect of change, since knowledge gives you the power to modify your behavior. In the following exercise I want you to determine all of the constructive, and destructive, habits you have acquired from your parents. (This is an excellent exercise to share with your working partner, as your blind spots might interfere with your self-assessment.)

List as many as you can. You might want to use a separate notebook for many of these exercises. The following is an example:

Constructive Acquired Habits
- Personal hygiene
- Discipline
- Good manners
- Sincerity

Destructive Acquired Habits

- Worry
- Low self-esteem
- Bad habits
- Procrastinate
- Temper

The above is just a sampling to give you an idea of what I want you to look for. The objective of this exercise is twofold. You will more fully understand role model empowerment, and you will begin to break away from habits that might be holding you back, and focus on your strengths.

Constructive Acquired Habits

_____

_____

_____

_____

Destructive Acquired Habits

_____

_____

_____

_____

High achievers

Behind every high achiever is usually a positive role model. You can refer to this person(s) as a mentor, hero, confidant, mother, father . . . the label is not important. The critical realization is that significant personal and professional growth is often stimulated by identifying with a hero, a role model.

Do you have a hero? Do you have a role model? Were your parents a constructive or destructive influence in the acquired habits you currently possess? What about your working partner?

My observation has been—tragic as it is—that most adults go through life without heroes. Most people do not have a positive role model. If I may suggest, could this be why so few salespeople ever scratch the surface of their God-given potential? I think it merits serious consideration.

Most salespeople, just like most students, are trained by the book. Rote learning is emphasized and rewarded in the safe, structured environment of the classroom. But not so in the real world. Acquired role model habits are the difference between knowledge and performance.

Basketball superstar Michael Jordan patterned his game after two local basketball heros, David Thompson and Walter Davis. They were his inspiration to excel, to dunk, and to make it to the NBA. They served a valuable purpose in his life, and Michael Jordan is now a household personality, and a role model for millions!

General George Patton idolized Alexander The Great. As a youth, he studied everything ever written about his hero. When he was a cadet at West Point, he patterned his military learning and career after Alexander. When General Patton was in the heat of battle against the Nazis in Europe, all of his decisions were made with the consideration of how his role model, Alexander The Great, would have acted under similar circumstances. A cynic might say it's a coincidence that neither General lost a battle, but I respectfully disagree.

Inner Qualities vs Outer Qualities

In 1988, when my firm conducted the survey, albeit nonscientific, of 1700 salespeople, I discovered virtually nine out of ten salespeople could double their daily prospecting. My initial objective for conducting the survey was to determine what qualities and characteristics the typical salesperson thought were critical for achieving success.

This exercise was so enlightening, both to me and the salespeople surveyed, that I've since included it in many of my presentations to help illustrate role model empowerment. Let me now share it with you.

Working Partner Exercise:

Again, this exercise is to be shared with your working partner. In the spaces that follow the example below, identify your hero. This might not be easy for a person who has never had a hero. Think about that one person with whom you would gladly trade places. Dead or alive, it makes no difference. Actually, many people initially find it easier to select a hero from the history books, as General Patton did, than find a living role model. In a short while, you will be able to select a live role model, too.

After identifying your hero, list 24 qualities and characteristics that have contributed to his or her greatness. These can be everyday qualities such as confidence, discipline, etc. There is no reason for my asking you to select 24, other than it forces you to dig deep. In all high achievers, there is more than meets casual observation.

The following is a start:

HERO: Ben Franklin

Qualities and characteristics:

1. Discipline
2. Industrious
3. Practical
4. Honest
5. Persistent
6. Goal Focused
7.

The idea is to spend time reflecting on the special attributes that helped your hero become somebody special. No one quality or characteristic can stand alone for greatness; this is a synergy. A synergy is defined as, "the whole being greater than the sum of the individual parts." The power of these specific qualities is most visibly apparent when missing.

HERO: _____

Qualities and characteristics:

1 _____
2 _____
3 _____
4 _____
5 _____
6 _____
7 _____
8 _____
9 _____
10 _____
11 _____
12 _____

13 _____

14 _____

15 _____

16 _____

17 _____

18 _____

19 _____

20 _____

21 _____

22 _____

23 _____

24 _____

Now that you have identified all 24 qualities and characteristics of greatness in your hero, it's time to label them as inner qualities (IQ), or school qualities (SQ). Use the following as your working definition for this exercise:

INNER QUALITIES (IQ): Qualities and characteristics that have been developed through life. These are basically attributable to living and growing outside of the classroom. Example: Discipline is an IQ.

SCHOOL QUALITIES (SQ): This is textbook knowledge. The information you were fed by a teacher, in a classroom, and tested on. Much of product knowledge can be considered SQ, along with your ability to spell. Example: Geometry is an SQ.

There will be some overlap as you label your hero's traits. This is only natural. When this happens, assign the most dominant label to the quality.

Upon completion of the labeling, compare the percentage of inner qualities to school qualities, IQ's vs SQ's. I have been amazed in many of my seminars when the participants label all of the qualities and characteristics that have contributed to the success of their heroes, as inner qualities, IQ's! The results of my survey were a little more modest, as the salespeople scored 92 percent as inner qualities.

There is much hidden value in this hero labeling. Not only did you have to identify with a hero, a role model, you then had to focus on what really contributed to his or her success. What is less obvious, subconsciously you have already been comparing your qualities and characteristics to those of your heroes.

You can relate very easily to many of these qualities because they are so natural. Did you list a Ph.D. from Harvard or Yale as a major contributor? Probably not.

People are taken back by the requirements, in their own estimation, for high level achievement. Most of these requirements are not taught in a classroom. Most do not require a genius level intelligence. What is so encouraging to salespeople, as I teach these principles throughout the country, is that the opportunity for high level achievement is available for all who are willing.

All those inner qualities are very natural and can be developed by taking control of your internal tapes and your self-image. Simple, but not easy. This is the essence of winning the inner game of selling.

A challenge

Most large companies do not understand the rules of success. They are brainwashed by titles, degrees and fancy packaging. I can remember conducting a long-term inner game achievement group with 15 of the top producers in a large brokerage firm. Everything was moving along very well, and I had sent a memo around to the participants that the next session would focus on referrals. I also sent a copy to upper management.

The morning of my session, I got a note from the receptionist that the vice president of marketing wanted to see me. As I walked into his office, he nodded for me to sit down and picked up a copy of my correspondence. Without making eye contact with me he said, "Matt, I'm hearing very good things about your program, the brokers seem to like it. However, we don't need to be wasting any of our money on teaching these people how to generate referrals. We've got the best referral- generating program in the business, and I have personally trained every broker in this firm. We're paying you to teach the principles of the inner game of selling. Let's stick to it!"

He did not even allow me to respond. He simply smiled, shook my hand, and left me to conduct my program. Well, not only did he get my dander up, he raised my curiosity concerning the broker's use of his referral program.

I asked the group if they were actively generating referrals. None were. I asked them if they knew how, and all replied that they did. I then shared my discussion with the vice president with the group. They all had a laugh. Apparently they'd all received similar monologues at one time or another, and didn't seem to hold much regard for their

VP's opinions. They urged me to go forward with my program on generating referrals. So we did.

Results

When we met three weeks later, everyone had a list of active referrals. One broker had gotten 147 referrals from his existing clients, simply by calling and asking for them.

The magic was recognizing that the IQ's were holding them back, not the knowledge. The vice president was partially correct; they had the knowledge, but it was being wasted without the understanding of the IQ's.

Knowledge is not power; it's the application of knowledge that is true power. Your inner qualities will allow you to apply the knowledge and skills you currently possess. Why learn more until you're applying what you already know?

What Is A Role Model?

Does your role model have to be perfect? Of course not! Only after Michael Jordan achieved much of his success through a combination of natural talent and acquired habits, did he realize that both of his role models had serious problems with drugs and alcohol.

Alexander The Great had many wives, but his real love was a man closer to the age of his father. When his gentleman lover died, Alexander The Great followed soon after by drinking himself to death.

Like Michael Jordan and General George Patton, identify with only the qualities and characteristics of your role model that are important to your goals and aspirations.

People find it very comforting when they realize that their role model was not perfect. In many cases, their role model had significant flaws, but by focusing on strengths, they were still able to achieve. You are probably more similar to your role model than you are different. They are human, their weaknesses are human; they are just like you.

Active and passive role models

There are two types of role models. General Patton had a passive role model in Alexander The Great. Alexander had an active role model in his private tutor, Aristotle.

Active Role Model: an individual with whom you have regular contact. Like Aristotle to Alexander, questions could be directly asked and answered, behavior directly observed and modeled.

38

Passive Role Model: an individual who is studied from a distance. Whether alive or dead, there is no direct contact, and all information has to be gathered second hand.

History books play a major role in gathering passive role model information. Do not concern yourself so much with the accuracy of your information; you're not attempting to be a historian. The importance is your belief in your role model.

Some people are fortunate enough to have both active and passive role models. Frank Bettger, who wrote the best selling book, *How I Raised Myself From Failure To Success In Selling,* was a failure at the age of 29. Then, he became one of America's highest paid salespeople at the age of 40. Frank Bettger patterned his career as a life insurance agent using two role models who had nothing to do with insurance. But they epitomized success!

His active role model was Dale Carnegie. Bettger learned much from his mentor, and most importantly, allowed himself to be continually pushed to new heights. Carnegie not only helped him develop the necessary IQ's to become a successful salesman, he challenged him to write a book and give speeches. Bettger was equal to the task, excelling in each instance.

But Dale Carnegie was not the only positive influence in Frank Bettger's life. He also had a passive role model, Benjamin Franklin. Upon discovering a prayer that Franklin authored and recited daily, Bettger began repeating the same words daily. His reasoning was, "If that prayer helped Ben Franklin, it certainly ought to help me."

Frank Bettger also followed Franklin's 13-week self-study program for acquiring certain virtues. This involved determining 13 qualities he considered important, and committing one week to concentrate on each specific quality. In this fashion, Franklin was able to give priority attention to each quality four separate weeks each year. It was his quarterly self-help system. The current self-help movement could learn a thing or two from Mr. Franklin!

Thirteen qualities and characteristics of high achievers

You are now going to evaluate yourself, your working partner, and your role model against what I've found to be the 13 most critical ingredients common to high achievers.

These 13 qualities and characteristics were not selected at random. They were the result of over one thousand hours of studying the lives of successful people, coupled with my work with human behavior, and the survey we conducted in 1988.

This list is by no means inclusive; please feel free to adjust it as you see fit.

I must admit I zeroed in on the number 13 because of my passive role model, Ben Franklin. It is a good way of utilizing the quarterly system if you break it down into weeks, and it also eliminates superstition. Ha!

Qualities and Characteristics of High Achievers

Note: Circle the number most applicable, with *one being the least* and *ten the most.*

1. *Goal Focused:* High achievers have a strong sense of purpose and work their life from a specific plan. They control as much as they can. (You must do the same.)

   Role Model: 1 2 3 4 5 6 7 8 9 10

   Working Partner: 1 2 3 4 5 6 7 8 9 10

   You: 1 2 3 4 5 6 7 8 9 10

2. *Confident:* Complete belief in their ability, often without proof, to achieve their goals.

   Role Model: 1 2 3 4 5 6 7 8 9 10

   Working Partner: 1 2 3 4 5 6 7 8 9 10

   You: 1 2 3 4 5 6 7 8 9 10

3. *High Self-Esteem:* High achievers focus on their strengths and truly like themselves. They are free from nagging self-criticism.

   Role Model: 1 2 3 4 5 6 7 8 9 10

   Working Partner: 1 2 3 4 5 6 7 8 9 10

   You: 1 2 3 4 5 6 7 8 9 10

4. *Success Self-Image:* These people had the ability to see themselves as successful well in advance of their actual achievements. Their self-image was in harmony with their goals.

Role Model: 1 2 3 4 5 6 7 8 9 10

Working Partner: 1 2 3 4 5 6 7 8 9 10

You: 1 2 3 4 5 6 7 8 9 10

5. *Discipline and Achievement:* All high achievers had the magic of self-motivation; this is a discipline. Coupled with achievement drive, success follows.

Role Model: 1 2 3 4 5 6 7 8 9 10

Working Partner: 1 2 3 4 5 6 7 8 9 10

You: 1 2 3 4 5 6 7 8 9 10

6. *Role Modeled:* An active ongoing modeling of themselves after successful people, and becoming a role model.

Role Model: 1 2 3 4 5 6 7 8 9 10

Working Partner: 1 2 3 4 5 6 7 8 9 10

You: 1 2 3 4 5 6 7 8 9 10

7. *Empowerment:* High achievers traditionally bring out the best in the people around them, by helping them believe in themselves.

Role Model: 1 2 3 4 5 6 7 8 9 10

Working Partner: 1 2 3 4 5 6 7 8 9 10

You: 1 2 3 4 5 6 7 8 9 10

8. *Self-Awareness:* Ben Franklin created 13 virtues out of his awareness of strengths and weaknesses.

Role Model: 1 2 3 4 5 6 7 8 9 10

Working Partner: 1 2 3 4 5 6 7 8 9 10

You: 1 2 3 4 5 6 7 8 9 10

9. *Self-Managed:* Achievers manage their time well, providing pri-oritized order in their lives.

   Role Model: 1 2 3 4 5 6 7 8 9 10

   Working Model: 1 2 3 4 5 6 7 8 9 10

   You: 1 2 3 4 5 6 7 8 9 10

10. *Pro-Active:* These people accept responsibility for their plans, and act! Procrastination is not in their being.

   Role Model: 1 2 3 4 5 6 7 8 9 10

   Working Partner: 1 2 3 4 5 6 7 8 9 10

   You: 1 2 3 4 5 6 7 8 9 10

11. *Persistent:* Ben Franklin termed it resolution, finishing what you start, and working diligently, day after day.

   Role Model: 1 2 3 4 5 6 7 8 9 10

   Working Partner: 1 2 3 4 5 6 7 8 9 10

   You: 1 2 3 4 5 6 7 8 9 10

12. *Health and Fitness:* High level energy is required for high level achievement, as there is no time for illness or needless fatigue.

   Role Model: 1 2 3 4 5 6 7 8 9 10

   Working Partner: 1 2 3 4 5 6 7 8 9 10

   You: 1 2 3 4 5 6 7 8 9 10

13. *Courage:* Nothing ventured, nothing gained is the motto for achievers. They take risks and are willing to fail in order to ulti-mately succeed. Winston Churchill said it so well, "Courage is the first of human qualities because it is the quality which guarantees all the others."

   Role Model: 1 2 3 4 5 6 7 8 9 10

   Working Partner: 1 2 3 4 5 6 7 8 9 10

   You: 1 2 3 4 5 6 7 8 9 10

I could easily have included some other essential qualities, such as balanced living, strong values, as well as a host of others, but this list is more comprehensive than it might appear. Remember, the objective is to identify the human qualities of you, your role model and your working partner. The strongest results will come your way by allowing your partnership to jointly determine what is most important for your ultimate success as a salesperson and as a human being. This eliminates any blind spots.

Allow yourself to recapture some of the natural learning qualities of an infant. Reflect on a little toddler just learning how to walk, taking those first couple of steps. How many of the 13 qualities and characteristics are applicable in this primary growth step? A strong argument can be made for all 13.

Wrap-Up

- Most accelerated learning and growth is from role models.
- Parents are your initial role model.
- Roles models can be either constructive or destructive.
- Many of your habits have been acquired from your parents.
- Share your acquired habits with your working partner.
- Identify a hero, a role model.
- Ninety percent or more, of the qualities and characteristics of most role models are inner qualities—IQ's.
- IQ is a quality or characteristic that was learned outside of the classroom.
- SQ is a school quality taught by a teacher out of a book.
- There are two types of role models: active and passive.
- Understand your strengths relative to your role model and working partner concerning the 13 qualities.
- Work jointly with your working partner to avoid blind spots.

IMPORTANT STUFF!

1. List below the stuff you found important in this chapter.

_____

_____

2. What do you want to change? _____

_____

_____

3. When are you going to change it? _____

_____

_____

4. What are you going to enhance?_____

_____

_____

5. How are you going to enhance it? _____

_____

_____

Chapter 5

THE POWER OF BALANCED PERSONAL GROWTH

As you and your working partner prepare to embark on your success journey, you must realize that winning the inner game of selling involves a lot more than just making large sums of money. Your ultimate long-term earnings will flow from your inner accomplishments. The salesperson who is absorbed by his or her commission statement will have, at best, short-lived satisfaction.

Your lasting professional success in sales requires a commitment to ongoing personal growth in all areas of your life. Therefore, it's extremely important to strive to become a complete human being; a superior person (family member, neighbor, associate, friend), as well as a superior salesperson. This is what winning the inner game of selling is all about—the total you!

The Total You

If you want to maximize your potential, you cannot limit your efforts to only one segment of your life. You must approach life as a whole. Imagine a chair with only one good leg, and you will get the concept. It's impossible to separate one part of your life from another. The chair needs four good legs, a seat, and a back to function as it should.

As simple and basic as this concept appears, the world is full of people who fail to recognize how all aspects of their life are interconnected. A common example is the salesman who justifies a near-poverty lifestyle by saying, "My family is very important to me, and I want to be home for dinner every night." Really, is his family better off just because Daddy's home every night, even though there's not enough money to buy school clothes for the kids? Or, is this a one-legged chair?

One of the best definitions of success, so eloquent the words paint a picture of both the need for achievement and balance, was written many years ago by Robert Louis Stevenson. Read his passage out loud, allow your imagination to see the pictures Stevenson has painted, and place these words of yesterday into your world of today. You might want this passage visible, fixed on a wall in your office to read every day.

Achievement

"That man is a success who has lived well, laughed often and loved much; who has gained the respect of intelligent men and the love of children; who has filled his niche and accomplished his task; who leaves the world better than he found it, whether by improved poppy, a perfect poem or a rescued soul; who never lacked appreciation of earth's beauty or failed to express it; who looked for the best on others and gave the best he had."

Is this really success?

I recently had an individual visit me at my private practice who couldn't stop talking about what a superstar salesman he was. This man, who I'll refer to as Fred, was 45 years of age. He told me all about his two large houses, his boat, the three luxury cars, etc.

Almost as an aside he began to talk about the purpose of his visit; failed marriage, recurring headaches, alcohol problem, temper, stress and about 100 pounds of extra weight.

It didn't take a trained counselor to determine that this guy was a walking-talking disaster. He was a death-trap waiting to spring. But, when I suggested that he had to completely "buy-in" to a behavioral lifestyle change, he balked saying: "I've already succeeded, I've got everything. I don't think I need to buy-in to any more accomplishments."

Who would consider him a success? His children, his ex-wife? I doubt it! Yet how often do we forget ourselves and try to keep score, using only money as the measuring device? I wonder what Fred's physician has to say about his success?

Family and religion

A friend of mine chose to use his family, and later religion, to justify his lower-middle class standard of living. Before I was blessed with children, Ralph used to give me lectures about his devotion to family. He claimed it kept him from pursuing his career with the same focus that I did.

Shortly after I became a father, Ralph found religion. I now became the subject of lectures on faith, as he had become totally immersed with church functions. We have little contact any more. I guess we just grew apart. I have my family, my church, and my professional career. Ralph has his justification for his modest income.

Most high achievers, as evidenced in the IQ/SQ exercise, are well rounded and full of spiritual goodness. They have an equal commitment to family, God, charity, and their profession. There's a freedom, a spiritual congruence, a committing of self to total excellence as a human being.

Putting everything into perspective

Winning the inner game of selling requires balance. Living with sound spiritual values doesn't require you to ignore the rest of your life, any more than maintaining a loving relationship with your spouse and children demands your presence at home every evening. This means that you do not have to sacrifice fulfillment in one area for achievement in another.

Balanced living is actually very self-descriptive. Paying attention to your health and fitness is an important step towards maximizing your income. Likewise, it's a proven fact that people who have good relationships at home are more effective in their chosen professions.

Your working partner is a member of this support team. This person will compliment your family unit. And, in cases of single professionals, he or she will act as your family relationship support.

Working Partner Exercise:

You are about to graph your life from your earliest remembrances to the present. This is a fascinating exercise that needs to be completed with your working partner. This is also a frightening exercise for many people. You will, perhaps for the first time, allow someone to really know you. If you have never done anything like this before, I am excited for you. It's worth it, it can change your life. In my 15 years of working with human behavior, I have never witnessed an activity that bonded people together with the same combination of speed and strength.

By sharing with your working partner the specific highs and lows of your life, you will become exposed. And, through this vulnerability you will realize that you have a lot in common. You will experience, on a highly emotional level, the feeling, not just the understanding, that people are more similar than dissimilar.

The following is the life map of a 52-year-old life insurance agent; I'll call him Tom Abrams. Tom is very successful and has been earning well into six figures for as long as he can remember.

Tom Abrams' Life Map

Highs

- ★ Father took me to a ball game when I was four.
- ★ Had my first girlfriend in third grade, we used to hold hands walking to our school.
- ★ I made the freshman basketball team.
- ★ I loved school; I was a good student; it was my escape.
- ★ Went to college and got away from home!
- ★ Graduated from college and got married.
- ★ Started my selling career.
- ★ Made MDRT at age 29.
- ★ Birth of my daughter.
- ★ CLU designation.
- ★ ChFC designation.
- ★ Three-week family cruise.
- ★ Sharing and helping "hungry" agents.

Lows

- I felt abandoned on my first day in kindergarten.
- My father used to beat me.
- I can remember being afraid when I saw him walking up the sidewalk; I used to hide.
- I realized my father was an alcoholic when he was drunk at my basketball games.
- Mother finally left my father, but the damage was done.
- Ran out of money in college; father lost his job and I had to take one year off to work.

Tom Abram's Life Map Graph

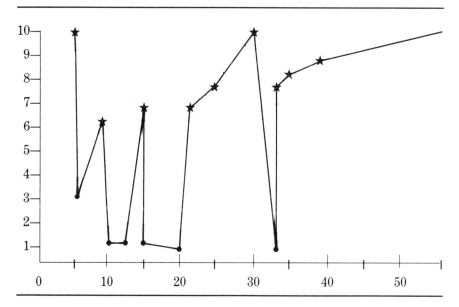

Soon it will be your turn. How do you feel? Are you out of your comfort zone? Is your working partner? I was, during my first exposure to his powerful exercise!

Before we really get started, let me share just one of my lows with you, as an example.

I am flashing back to my senior year in high school. Even though many years have past, I can't express the feeling that comes over me as I share this particular low point. My best description is a hybrid of shame and growth. Only by sharing my shame was I able to experience true growth. Please keep in mind, it's your perception of an experience, the guilt, anger, shame, etc., that is important to recognize, not the outward severity. What I'm about to share with you was traumatic to me.

Back to my story. During the fall of my senior year I got suspended from high school for being drunk at a school dance. The suspension didn't really bother me because in my juvenile mind, everybody was drinking, I just happened to get caught. My trauma came from facing my mother. A large group of us had been suspended the previous year for the same infraction. (We really weren't drunks; no one developed an alcohol problem, we just had more hormones than sense.) At the time, I promised my mother that it would never happen again. Yes, she could trust me. . . .

My shame was looking into the teary eyes of my mother as she asked only one question. "Why?" she stammered. I couldn't answer, so choked up with guilt and emotion I knew I would cry if I spoke. Silence was all I could muster. To which my mother gave me a lecture about trust, faith and life. I will never forget that scene; all I wanted to do was to crawl into a hole and die.

My growth came from emotionally buying into the importance of trust and integrity. Only years later did I realize, through sharing this experience, that I had used this humiliating episode to change the direction of my life. It didn't automatically transform me from bad to good, rather it was an evolutionary process. But it played a role in making me the person I am today.

Now it's your turn.

Feel free to use your own notebook if you want more space. First list the highs and lows, as you can remember them, in your life. List them in chronological order, and graph them accordingly.

Highs

_____

_____

_____

_____

_____

_____

_____

Lows

_____

_____

_____

_____

_____

_____

_____

Your Life Map Graph

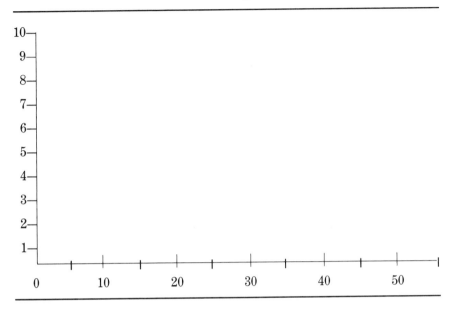

Now that you've shared your history with your working partner, you're ready to design your future. Up to this point in your life you haven't actually had control. You probably didn't plan your life map as you just graphed it with your partner. You would have changed a few things, wouldn't you? I know that I would!

The second phase of your life map is the fun part. From this point forward, you will control your life. You are going to design your future.

Making up your future life map

Are you ready to make up the rest of your life? You are going to carry your life map out as far as you can take it. You will be looking at your life as a continuum, from right now to death—for this is what you can control. How long do you see yourself living?

After you project how long you would like to live, determine three personal and three professional accomplishments that you would like to achieve before you die.

I know, it's difficult to be considering your own death. But let's face it, as certain as night follows day, we are all going to die. The objective is not to dwell on death, but rather plan what you are going to accomplish during your life. Considering death helps eliminate procrastination.

Your life as a continuum

Answer the following questions before you begin to consider your major personal and professional accomplishments.

- How would you like to be remembered by your children?
- How would like to be remembered by your co-workers?
- How would you like to be remembered by your community?
- How would you like to be remembered by your friends?
- How would you like to be remembered by your clients?
- How do you wanted to be viewed spiritually?

Only after carefully addressing each of those six questions, and imagining the response you would like, can you legitimately create your life map. People who have had near-death experiences all describe a similar story; a very peaceful feeling, travelling through a tunnel with a beam of light at the end. Upon reaching the end of the tunnel, they see their entire life flash in front of them in vivid detail. They focus on their relationships, parents they wish they had expressed more love to, a spouse who they wish they had been nicer to, etc.

What do you really want to contribute during the rest of your life? Again, I've limited this exercise to three major personal and professional accomplishments to force you to focus and prioritize. This is a powerful exercise. If you don't have enough room to write your accomplishments in the spaces below, use your notebook.

Life's Continuum

NOW (AGE) _____

DATE _____

Major Personal Accomplishments

1. _____

2. _____

3. _____

Major Professional Accomplishments

1. _____

2. _____

3. _____

DEATH (AGE) _____

What went through your mind as you observed your life as a continuum? Have you ever done such an exercise? Most people express a myriad of emotions. During my seminars the conversation usually takes on another dimension, more significance, more depth, following this exercise.

Your top priorities

As you developed your future life map, serious consideration was given to your upcoming accomplishments. The next step is to focus your thoughts on what's most important to you, personally and professionally.

Aside from your working partner, you can gather input from your spouse and children at this point. (It amazes me how many people have trouble communicating with their family. This would be a fine start.)

Your immediate commitment is going to center around your top-priority personal and professional accomplishments. Therefore, you will have two major focal points. Points that will impact every part of your life.

Work with your partner as you zero in on these priorities. Without this steadying influence, you may become overwhelmed by your planned future, and you may lose all sense of control. Some people take hours, or days, to come up with their priorities. Take all of the time you need. You are establishing the meaning of your life and, of course, your relationship to selling.

Recently I took my car in for a regular tune-up and oil change. The mechanic, apparently looking over my car as he wrote the job order, informed me that my front tires were bald.

"What!", I cried, "they're less than six months old!" To which I was informed that my car's front end was out of balance. Ouch! In addition to the cost of regular maintenance, I was hit with a front end alignment, brakes, and tires. But the worst part was my ignorance. I was totally unaware my car was out of balance.

Fortunately, it was only my car. I counsel people everyday in similar predicaments with their lives. Ignorance is bliss only until it bites you. My car bit me for a bill four times what I was anticipating. Your life can bite you in many ways—burnout, depression, alcohol/drugs, divorce, illness. . .

So let's take a quick inventory of the balance in your life. The following profile cannot cover everything, but it will provide you with a good working start. For those who want to pursue this further, and I recommend that you do, write to the National Wellness Institute, South Hall, University of Wisconsin-Stevens Point, Stevens Point, Wisconsin, 54481, (715)-346-2172, and ask about their Lifestyle Assessment Questionnaire. It is an excellent tool!

BLP: Balanced Living Profile

	Strongly Agree	Mildly Agree	Mildly Disagree	Strongly Disagree
1. I enjoy my work.	1	2	3	4
2. My work is challenging.	1	2	3	4
3. My values guide my personal and professional life.	1	2	3	4
4. I feel good about my spiritual life.	1	2	3	4
5. I spend a sufficient amount of time with my family.	1	2	3	4
6. I share my true feelings with my spouse (significant other).	1	2	3	4
7. I make a conscious effort to eat nutritional foods at every meal.	1	2	3	4
8. I am healthy and maintain my ideal weight.	1	2	3	4
9. I seldom let a rough day at work affect my attitude at home.	1	2	3	4
10. I read twelve or more books a year.	1	2	3	4
11. I watch less than 10 hours of television per week.	1	2	3	4
12. I attend religious services weekly.	1	2	3	4
13. I find satisfaction from my work.	1	2	3	4
14. My work contributes to my personal needs and overall well-being.	1	2	3	4
15. I am a good role model at home, work, and in society in general.	1	2	3	4

Maximum Score = 60   My Score ＿＿＿＿＿＿

Score

60 — 54	You are out of whack! Regardless of your accomplishments, you're taking years off your life. Take special care in developing your "Mission Statement."
53 — 43	You are in the danger zone. Pay close attention to all facets of your life as you develop your "Mission Statement."
42 — 30	You can improve. Target specific areas that will give you more balance.
29 — 22	You are doing well! A little fine-tuning will do wonders.
21 —	Fantastic lifestyle! Prepare for ongoing personal and professional growth.

Areas For Improvement:

Review the individual items on the Profile and determine specific areas that you need to develop, strengthen, and enhance in your efforts to eliminate procrastination and improve performance. If you:

Circled **4,** you've identified an area to **develop.**

Circled **3,** you've identified an area to **strengthen.**

Circled **2,** you've identified an area to **enhance.**

Select *three areas* to work on between now and your next group meeting. List them below and discuss them with your partner.

#1— ＿＿＿＿＿＿＿＿＿＿＿＿＿＿＿＿＿＿＿＿＿＿＿＿＿＿＿＿＿

#2— ＿＿＿＿＿＿＿＿＿＿＿＿＿＿＿＿＿＿＿＿＿＿＿＿＿＿＿＿＿

#3— ＿＿＿＿＿＿＿＿＿＿＿＿＿＿＿＿＿＿＿＿＿＿＿＿＿＿＿＿＿

Your mission statement: values to live by

I feel certain that you now have a better understanding about your meaning in life. Right? It tends to be a philosophical topic, but the salespeople who can succinctly determine this meaning are usually the winners.

Your personal mission statement requires the same attention you placed on your life map. Once again, I'm asking you to go deep within yourself. You are creating the rules, the values, by which you are going be guided through your life.

Try to keep your sentences short and specific as you cover the following areas: family, professional, spiritual, personal and health.

Mission Statement Guideline

(Think in terms of one to three sentences per area.)

FAMILY:

1. _____

_____

_____

2. _____

_____

_____

3. _____

_____

_____

PROFESSIONAL:

1. _____

_____

_____

2. _____

_____

_____

3. _____

_____

_____

SPIRITUAL:

1. _____
_____
_____

2. _____
_____
_____

3. _____
_____
_____

PERSONAL:

1. _____
_____
_____

2. _____
_____
_____

3. _____
_____
_____

HEALTH:

1. _____
_____
_____

2. _____
_____
_____

3. _____
_____
_____

By writing one to three sentences for each of the above you have started to craft a mission statement that will describe what your life plan is all about. Most people need a few re-writes to get everything in place, so don't feel pressured to come up with a polished work of art.

Now, try putting it all together as one flowing statement. Clarity and simplicity are good guidelines to follow. Try to keep your statement to one sheet of paper; a couple of paragraphs is ideal.

Your personal mission statement

_____

_____

_____

_____

_____

_____

_____

_____

_____

_____

_____

_____

_____

_____

_____

_____

_____

_____

_____

Review your statements with your working partner. Make certain that you both agree that they represent the life you want to live, and the person you want to be, as you embark on your inner game success journey. This is your personal statement of life. It identifies you as a person to yourself. You now have established your meaning of life.

Family mission statement

For those of you who have families, call a family meeting and develop a family mission statement if you want to bring magic into your household. Young children, nine years old and up, can be included. The younger ones will have to wait a few years before they take on the responsibility for establishing family rules.

The object of involving your children in this mission statement is simple; when they have input on what is required of them, they feel a much greater sense of responsibility to carry out their part—they have an "equity position" in the family.

Part of our family mission involves my daughter Heidi. Even though she's only eight years old, she has determined that she could be responsible for picking up her clothes, brushing her teeth, bathing herself, clearing her plate and putting it into the dishwasher, and answering all telephone calls.

Occasionally, Heidi needs some reminding about all of the above, except answering the telephone. In fact, she was so determined to answer the phone, that she would race to the phone and answer with an out of breath "Hey!" We revised the contract. She would be the designated telephone answerer in our family, but she had to always answer the phone with "Hello, this is Heidi."

Heidi did slip a few times and forget. But within a week, she was answering the phone just as we had agreed. Heidi felt an ownership to that agreement. She helped construct the rules, and subsequently finds it very natural to answer the phone accordingly.

If you develop a family mission statement. Consider the following:

• How does your family perceive itself as a unit?
• How would you ideally like your family unit to be?
• What are your responsibilities?
• What are your spouse's responsibilities?
• What are each child's responsibilities?

This is more involved than your personal statement because it builds on it, involving input from your family members. You need to have dialogue at each step of the way. If your children consider it your responsibility to spend Saturday with the family, rather than on the golf course, and your wife agrees with them, you must work out an acceptable compromise that is agreeable to all.

Everyone must have input. Everyone will have to assume certain responsibilities to ensure the family is the functioning unit everyone wishes it to be. You will be amazed with how responsive your children will be, and how much they will understand. If you're wondering what this has to do with your success in selling, let me remind you that the more supportive your family, the more you will achieve. Yes, it will require an investment of time. But it will be one of the best investments you will ever make.

Once you have your family mission statement written, get it typed and place it somewhere visible for all to see. Also, have each one of your children write their responsibilities and post them in their room.

A few last thoughts

Whether it's your personal or family mission statement, imagine someone reading it and ask yourself: "Does this statement explain what I am, or my family is, really about?" If it does, you have a true mission statement. If you sense there are some grey areas, you need to do some re-writing.

Always word all of your sentences in the present tense positive. It's important to word your mission statement as your ideal, as if it were true now.

Take your time, write and word carefully, and make your personal mission statement your "Bylaws" of life. Your responsibility is to "buy-in" to your own statement. Go for it, it's easier than you think!

Wrap-Up

- To maximize your potential, to utilize all of your talents, a commitment must be made for balanced growth.
- By sharing where you've been, highs and lows, you can determine where you want to go.
- Your life is a continuum; you will be remembered by your contributions—personally and professionally.
- Personal and professional growth must occur in tandem to have long-term value. Determine your top priorities in both areas.
- Your personal mission statement signifies the values that you live by.
- A family mission statement empowers a family through communication and responsibility.

IMPORTANT STUFF!

1. List below the stuff you found important in this chapter.

_____

_____

2. What do you want to change? _____

_____

_____

3. When are you going to change it? _____

_____

_____

4. What are you going to enhance?_____

_____

_____

5. How are you going to enhance it? _____

_____

_____

Chapter 6

ACTIVITY DRIVES THE DREAM

You've already laid the foundation for high achievement in every part of your life. Your personal mission statement is providing the rules and the values which you've established for this wonderful success journey. Now it's time for "the rubber to meet the road."

Everybody has dreams, but only a handful of people are able to translate their dreams into reality. There are many reasons for this—some you already know, others you are yet to discover. One of the major stumbling blocks for so many people with good intentions is nonactivity, the failure to DO.

Have you ever encountered a salesperson who loved to talk about his dreams, how he was going to really "tear it up this year," but never seemed able to act? He just couldn't put everything together. Many people can get temporarily excited about dreams they have for their future. But, all too frequently, they lose this enthusiasm when it comes to performing the daily activities that actually drive that dream. They only want the rewards, and overlook paying the price.

Consider the example of Mary.

Mary was an overweight sales rep with a large advertising agency. She was very articulate and began our first session by saying, "I'm very good at what I do. I know I could be even better, but I think being self-conscious about my weight is holding me back. I understand your concepts from the speech I heard you deliver to our local chamber of commerce. Please help me. I'll do anything!"

Mary certainly appeared to know what she wanted. She was well versed at describing what was holding her back. After a short interview, I discovered that even though she was good at sales, she could probably still double her income by mastering the inner game.

She agreed, and together we decided to approach her growth on two fronts; health and fitness, and selling. Mary's eating habits were poor. In fact, they could be interpreted as grazing. She had no structured eating schedule . . . snacked all day . . . ate a huge late dinner . . . snacked afterwards . . . and got no exercise. This pattern had to be changed. She was using it as an excuse for her poor self-image and marginal job performance.

We determined two specific activities that would support health and fitness:

1. To eat three balanced meals daily;
2. Walk 30 minutes or more daily.

Mary was only making between three to five calls per day. With a little time management, Mary figured she could consistently make seven to ten calls every day. Her sales commitment was:

1. Spend 8:00 a.m. to 9:30 a.m. on the phone setting seven to ten appointments;
2. Visit three to five prospects, or accounts, daily.

Upon returning for her next appointment one week later, Mary started in with her excuses: "I don't know why my life is so hectic! I had the best intentions of eating three meals a day, but you just wouldn't believe my schedule! I had to spend half the week just babying one account! Out to dinner, the whole bit. No time for lunch, no time for phone calls. Maybe the timing is not right for this," she whispered in conclusion.

Accountability vs talk

Mary could articulate her vision, intellectually she understood the rules of the game, but she couldn't, or wouldn't, carry out simple activities that would lead her to success. When she returned for her third visit her self-esteem was at an all time low. Why? She still wasn't carrying out her specific activities! These were action steps that she helped select, that she had determined she wanted to commit to.

Surprisingly, I was the first person to ever hold her accountable.

"Nobody's ever talked to me like you," she said, avoiding eye contact with me. "I guess I've been able to overwhelm everybody with my BS, but it's not doing me any good. Is it?"

I wish I could say Mary's a complete success story, but at this writing she's still working on her fixed activity. For the first time in her life, she's acting on what is within her control, rather than pontificating on what is not. Only time will tell if she really wants the success she speaks so eloquently about.

Can you relate to Mary? Many salespeople can. The best intentions and 50 cents will get you a cup of coffee—well, maybe a buck in metropolitan areas. Let's take a look at your future major accomplishments and do some prioritizing.

Top Priority Future Accomplishments

It's time to meet with your working partner and establish top priority personal and professional accomplishments. This will provide you with two targets to focus on.

Top priority personal accomplishment: _____

_____

Top priority professional accomplishment:

_____

Once you've established your two priority accomplishments, you'll want to determine what specific activities will drive these accomplishments. The objective is to keep everything simple—within your control. As you read the following question with your partner, give yourself some time for serious reflection, and write down two brief responses—one sentence per response. Answer this question twice—personally and professionally.

Activity Association Question: What two activities could you do (that you're currently not doing, or are doing poorly) that are completely in your control, that would play a major role in achieving each of your top priority accomplishments?

1. _____

2. _____

You'll find an activity commitment pledge later in the chapter. Until then, think of activities as you continue reading. I'll get back to this association game later.

Your life map—past, present, and future—will help you focus on what you really want. From there you can figure out what you need to do to succeed in this quest. I like to refer to these wants from your life map as dreams.

Your next step is to exercise your conscious will to determine the activities required to turn your dreams into reality. This becomes an internal management challenge, a discipline, because most of these activities are not glamorous or fun. They are hard work.

For example, making 25 prospecting calls every morning sounds simple to a stock broker who needs to make 150 calls a day. But it can appear overwhelming to an insurance agent who's only making five daily calls.

Sounds plain and simple, doesn't it? Identify what you want and manage your activities to achieve it.

Internal management

My first exposure to the real psychological makeup of sales people was as a young therapist in Worcester, Massachusetts. At the time I was busy trying to develop a name for myself with counseling. I was using therapeutic hypnosis as a primary modality. Back in those days there was little public awareness about hypnosis, and even less about its therapeutic value. My counseling practice was a real challenge.

Because my reputation preceded me (not as much for my wisdom, but rather because of the natural curiosity concerning hypnosis), many veteran salespeople visited my office. Most had experienced some level of success and were more versed in sales than I, but they had lost sight of their dream. As a result, many had lost much of their confidence and were suffering from various levels of low self-esteem.

My task was to get them to talk about themselves—easy to do when you're working with salespeople. I was equally fascinated and disturbed. Fascinated by the fact that most started their selling careers with visions of glory, tremendous enthusiasm, and a child-like belief in their abilities. Disturbed by such a total lack of all the wonderful qualities aforementioned; the dream, the enthusiasm, the beliefs were all gone.

What went wrong?

Dreams without a solid, well-managed action plan usually end up as wishful thinking. These salespeople, like so many others I've worked with over the years, never bothered to associate specific activities with attaining their dreams. Consequently, they never prioritized and managed the specific activities that would lead them, step by step, along that glorious path to success. They only concentrated on what was immediately pleasant. And, since most of the specific activities that needed daily attention weren't pleasant, they were put off. As a result, that glorious easy path to success had become a slow and depressing fight for survival. Individual comfort zones were shrinking, dreams of success and glory were turning into "pipe dreams," and the self-esteem and confidence, so essential to success, was rapidly vanishing.

By avoiding specific activities that might be viewed as unpleasant, boring or beneath them, these salespeople created an even more unpleasant situation—an unfulfilling life!

Imagine a farmer. He knows that simply dreaming of a plentiful harvest isn't going to produce anything. He's also aware that he can till a beautiful field and spend days planting his seeds, but if he doesn't tend his fields daily, he'll harvest only weeds.

This tending of the fields is probably the least exciting daily event for the farmer. It's really only necessary maintenance. Your specific daily activities are much the same. They aren't exciting. Frequently, they're the part of your job you dislike the most—prospecting, follow-up paperwork, asking for referrals. While none of this daily activity requires superior skills, it most definitely requires superior discipline, attitude and vision.

The bottom line is that most salespeople avoid what is unpleasant. This is why most are barely making a living. Usually it's those unpleasant activities that the heavy hitters do every day that drive their dreams. Your activities will drive your dreams!

Focus attention on what you can control

No matter how well trained, motivated, confident or internally programmed you might be, there is an unlimited array of external factors you can't control. Unfortunately, too many people focus on these events. They habitually fret over the weather, the stock market, interest rates, the exchange rate, foreign competition, etc.

You can't control the future achievements of your life map—sorry. But you can control how you prioritize and manage specific activities critical to these achievements.

Most people focus backwards

It just seems that too many people have been taught to do things backwards or outside-in.

Place yourself in Sara's shoes and try to relate to what happened to her. Sara had done everything right. She had received all the buying signals over a six-month period from a potential multimillion dollar prospect. When it was finally time to write some business, and she

67

was about to process the order, Mr. Frank, who was the purchasing agent for the large company, told Sara the deal was off.

Stunned, Sara struggled to ask for a reason. After some reluctance, and probably out of a feeling of guilt, this purchasing agent told Sara the truth, "I was all set to buy these PCs from you. Your price was right, I investigated your company and your reputation is excellent, and you are a true professional. I would like nothing more than to develop an ongoing relationship with you and your company. But, last week, when our senior vice president of finance was approving these major expenditures, he realized that his son-in-law was in the same business. He put his approval on hold, and two days later informed me we'd have the PCs shipped to us from his son-in-law. There's nothing I can do."

What can Sara do?

Sara lost this big sale because of circumstances completely out of her control. This happens all the time. It's a fact of life. It might not have been the son-in-law of a purchasing agent's boss, but how many times have you lost a deal because of external factors, events totally outside of your control?

Every professional salesperson has suffered through this experience, and will probably suffer again at some time. But there is nothing you can do. There was nothing Sara could do to change this purchasing agent's decision. But, she could control her response to the situation. Because she was so mortified, Sara failed to control her response and let opportunity slip through her fingers. She left without asking for any referrals!

This Sara could control. The deal was taken away from her by external factors. The purchasing agent was full of compliments and guilt about what happened. What a perfect time for Sara to take a deep breath, flush out the shock, and say, "You know I'm disappointed. I've worked extremely hard to put this deal together. We would have enjoyed a real win-win working relationship. But I understand, Mr. Frank, this is out of your control. But, in light of all that has occurred, would you do a favor for me?"

Unless this guy had a heart of stone, the answer would probably be, "I'd love to!"

Sara would then continue, "Do you know any other purchasing agents, Mr. Frank, whose companies use PCs, who would appreciate the same professional relationship we were about to begin? Would you call them and ask them to spend fifteen minutes with me?"

This hypothetical situation epitomizes the inner game of selling. Always focus on what you want, what you can control, and take action. In the example, Sara re-focused on what she could control. Although she had no control over the final purchase decision, and a cynic would claim bad luck, a salesperson committed to specific activities would be much more likely to get those referrals. This is what winning the inner game of selling is all about. Anybody can handle the good situations.

In evaluating this case with me, Sara learned a valuable lesson—to focus on activity she can control. She's now internally positioned to get the referrals regardless of external impact factors. How about you?

How long do you dwell on these external factors when they interfere? A few minutes was too long for Sara. It can be too long for you, too!

External and internal impact factors

Events totally out of your control will always impact your accomplishments, things such as sons-in-law, brothers-in-law, price, weather, death, delivery and competition. And, you have no control over them. Therefore, regardless of the impact, you don't have to waste time and energy worrying about them. Worry, unfortunately, becomes a pattern with many salespeople. By placing the blame for a lousy performance on external factors, failures are rationalized, and worry about the future becomes a built-in defense mechanism.

A basic law of the mind: *You think it, you live it!* Such was the case of these veteran salespeople who visited me early in my career. They'd become cynical underachievers who had lost their dream, their belief in self. They did this by focusing on problems, most of which were ultimately out of their control. They lacked the daily discipline of the farmer as they failed to tend to their fields.

But let's take a look at internal impact factors. These are activities completely within your control, and have a direct impact on your ultimate success. When I refer to internal and external impact factors, I'm talking about events within and outside of your control.

Internal impact factors: Specific activities, fixed behaviors, that are in your total control.

Example: Sara asking for referrals in the midst of rejection.

External impact factors: Anything that is out of your direct control.

Example: Vice president's son-in-law in the same business as Sara.

There's so much hype in typical sales training, many people believe that by simply saying the right words, having the right price, or convincing the prospect of a need, a sale will naturally follow. Not so in the real world!

Many salespeople have been brainwashed in their training. They feel that if they know all the "101" ways to handle objections, they should always get the sale. I've had salespeople question me during a workshop, "Shouldn't a real professional salesperson always be able to guide a qualified prospect into a buying decision?"

In theory, yes. It always works like that in the classroom when role playing or with the interactive video, but alas, as Sara can attest, theory and the real world are often light years apart.

The true professionals, working the phone lines and beating the streets in today's competitive world, know exactly what it takes to be successful. They understand their priorities and manage their time and activities accordingly. You need to have the same focus and understanding.

Working Partner Exercise:

The following is a partial list of some internal and external impact factors to assist you in this process. Go over it with your working partner. Determine what external factors you're going to stop worrying about, and the specific internal factors you're going to develop into your activity commitment. Understanding this difference will change your career!

Impact Factors

Internal

- Number of daily prospecting calls;
- Daily goal-setting exercise;
- Amount of preparation for a big dollar prospect;
- The quality, value and service you provide;
- Your continuing education —books, tapes, certification;
- Eating three well-balanced meals daily;
- Controlling your tapes.

External

- Number of prospects who are in;
- Date of accomplishment;
- The price—promises—of your competition;
- Son-in-law syndrome;
- "I'd love to do business with you but . . ."
- Attitude of your customers and prospects.

Most people quickly get the idea after looking over these comparisons. Share your own external impact factors with your working partner, but, please, don't dwell on them. Recognize them, evaluate your previous responses to them with your partner, then forget them and focus on the internal factors. These you can do something about!

Tactics

I'm asking you to develop and manage a strategic game plan. Your daily activity plan will be your specific strategic commitment. This will guarantee success. It just can't guarantee specifics.

Your tactics for getting what you want must center around what you can control. Only good things will happen to you and your partner as you hold each other accountable to predetermined daily activities.

Then, and only then, will you have accepted the responsibility for the "work" part of your success journey.

The Activities Drive the Dream

Let's get back to the activity association question at the beginning of the chapter. What are the stepping stones on your success journey? What activities must be attended to, day after day, in order to achieve those goals?

Let me repeat myself; this important consideration is frequently overlooked because it's just plain hard work. Few people are willing to pay the price. That's right! Far too many salespeople want all the trappings of success, but aren't willing to do anything different to earn it.

A good rule of thumb to follow is to ask yourself, "What does the typical salesman do on a Wednesday evening or Saturday morning?" Then do the opposite!

The typical traveling salesperson is in the cocktail lounge on the road (and you can bet that he is not looking for business either), or watching television. You must commit yourself to more constructive behavior. This is the price you must pay for success, and you must always pay in advance.

Well, let me give you your wake-up call. Your daily activities are your work load. They must be challenging, and you must get used to paying in advance. Make yourself uncomfortable every day!

There's nothing easy about making 35 telephone prospecting calls between 8 and 9:30 every morning. Yet, for many salespeople I work with, this is a requirement for success. How many daily prospecting calls need to be made to achieve the numbers necessary to drive your dream?

With your working partner, re-address the activity association question: What two activities could you do (that you're currently not doing or that you are performing poorly) that are completely in your control, that would play a major role in achieving your top priority accomplishment?

1. _____

2. _____

* NOTE: Answer this question twice; personally and professionally.

As I'm certain you understand by now, I want your attention focused on events you can totally control, internal impact factors. For many salespeople this points to the telephone. Ouch! Salespeople who interact with prospects most frequently are usually the most successful.

What are your specific activities?

What two specific activities have you decided to make yourself accountable for on a personal level? What two specific activities are you going to be accountable for on a professional level?

Your designated activities needn't be complex; in fact, the simpler the better. Let me give you some samples from a group of life insurance agents that I once worked with:

Professional:

Michael
1. Make 35 prospecting calls daily.
2. Ask for three referrals from all old and new clients.

Judy
1. Make 20 prospecting calls daily.
2. Set-up 15 appointments a week.

Personal:

Michael
1. Read for one hour daily.
2. Ride exercise bike 30 minutes daily.

Judy
1. Spend 30 minutes alone with each of her two children every day.
2. Read the Bible for 30 minutes every evening.

With your working partner, I want you to invest one full year to the principles of winning the inner game of selling—one year to your specific activities, your working partnership, your weekly meetings, your feedback, support and accountability. You'll be a living test of the validity of internal discipline.

For one year I want you concerned only with your internal impact factors. Let's make that commitment now.

YOUR ACTIVITY COMMITMENT   Date_____

In order to realistically achieve my top priority Professional Accomplishment of _____,

I _____, commit to holding myself daily accountable to the following two specific activities:

    1. _____

    _____

    2. _____

    _____

In order to realistically achieve my top priority Personal Accomplishment of_____

I, _____, commit to holding myself accountable to the following two specific activities:

    1. _____

    _____

    2. _____

    _____

Successful completion of these specific activities on a daily basis is essential to my success. I am accountable to myself and my working partner for the daily performance of these specific activities.

_____   _____
Signature   Date

_____   _____
Working Partner Signature   Date

Charting Your Activity

Even with the support of your working partner, all discipline is self-discipline. Just like all motivation is self-motivation and all true success is driven from within. You are the ultimate, and the only, person responsible for your behavior.

I have found over the years that keeping a weekly chart of activity posted in a highly visible location is extremely beneficial. Follow this simple four-step process:

1. At the close of every day write in your activity.

2. Mark a green dot on the days you do all of your professional activities. Use a blue dot to signal completion of personal activities. This should be done everyday. Use a felt marker; you'll be able to see the dots immediately on entering your office, and so will your working partner.

3. Reward yourself every day you complete your activities. Give yourself a treat, a workout at the health club, a silver dollar into a jar . . . anything to signify "good job today"!

4. Bring your charts to your weekly working partner meetings. File them weekly. These will become useful tools to determine trends and the best utilization of vacation times, etc.

Activity Chart

	ACTIVITY 1	ACTIVITY 2
SUNDAY		
MONDAY		
TUESDAY		
WEDNESDAY		
THURSDAY		
FRIDAY		
SATURDAY		
COMMENTS		

For some, procrastination is an occasional visitor; for others, a constant companion. In either case, it is a blockage to success that we can and need to conquer.

PAP: Procrastination Activity Profile

Instructions: This PAP Profile is geared to give you better insight into your relationship with activity. . . .

	Strongly Agree	Mildly Agree	Mildly Disagree	Strongly Disagree
1. I think I work better under pressure.	4	3	2	1
2. I find it difficult determining what to do first.	4	3	2	1
3. I find myself making excuses for unfinished work.	4	3	2	1
4. I often delay a task for so long that I'm embarrassed to to it.	4	3	2	1
5. I always make to-do lists for the upcoming day.	4	3	2	1
6. I lean toward perfection, always re-working a task even when it's good enough.	4	3	2	1
7. I put off my income tax form until April 1.	4	3	2	1
8. I feel frustrated much of the time.	4	3	2	1
9. I feel guilty when playing.	4	3	2	1
10. I use my time well.	1	2	3	4

Scoring the PAP: You will determine your PAP score by adding the numbers circled.

Maximum Score = 40   My Score _____

Score

40 — 36   You're a chronic procrastinator! Make certain to share this with your working partner. You need help!

35 — 29   You also need help. Get your working partner involved with your activity chart now.

28 — 21   Average. But this is not good enough for high achievement.

20 — 14   You are doing well. Make certain your partner keeps pace with you.

13 —   Give yourself a star! Now make your partner an efficiency expert too!

Areas For Improvement:

Review the individual items on the Profile and determine specific areas that you need to develop, strengthen, and enhance in your efforts to eliminate procrastination and improve performance. If you:

Circled **4,** you've identified an area to **develop.**

Circled **3,** you've identified an area to **strengthen.**

Circled **2,** you've identified an area to **enhance.**

Select *three areas* to work on between now and your next group meeting. List them below and discuss them with your partner.

#1— _____

#2— _____

#3— _____

Wrap-Up

- Give serious reflection to the Activity Association Question.
- Dreams without highly prioritized, specific activities turn into "pipe dreams."
- Always concentrate on what you can control.
- Internal impact factors are the fixed behaviors that have a direct effect on attaining your goals.
- Prioritizing these fixed behaviors will provide you with two activities per priority accomplishment to commit to.
- You must make a commitment to your activities—fill out the form!
- Fill out your activity chart daily, and discuss it weekly.
- Reward yourself daily for accomplishing your activities.

IMPORTANT STUFF!

1. List below the stuff you found important in this chapter.

    _____

    _____

2. What do you want to change? _____

    _____

    _____

3. When are you going to change it? _____

    _____

    _____

4. What are you going to enhance?_____

    _____

    _____

5. How are you going to enhance it? _____

    _____

    _____

Chapter 7

HOW TO RELAX AND WIN

Now that you've mapped out your future, prioritized your personal and professional accomplishments, and established specific activities to drive your dream, I want to share with you a concept that might strike you as a radical idea: *One of the most productive things you can do in selling is learn how to relax.* And, it's not as easy as you may think.

I will never forget the story that Linda, a life agent, shared with me about a large presentation she was giving to a mega-buck prospect. "I was so intimidated," she recalled, "that I was visibly perspiring. I became so self-conscious of this that I dropped my folder on the floor and knocked over a cup of coffee on the gentleman's desk. I was so embarrassed, I almost cried."

Fortunately, her story had a happy ending. Her prospect was a true gentleman and sympathized with her plight, and he allowed her to reschedule. Many salespeople aren't that fortunate. Millions of dollars in commissions are lost because of a severe case of nerves during a presentation.

Salespeople have become so action-oriented that they try to meet every quota and accomplish every goal by doing things. This is why so many salespeople feel as if they're spinning their wheels, moving fast, but getting nowhere. Gone is the time where anything can be accomplished with hard work alone.

In today's competitive marketplace, salespeople are awakening to the reality that more can be accomplished by working smart, by relaxing first, programming, and then acting. One of the most productive methods for doing this is the subject of this chapter. It's derived from therapeutic hypnosis and autohypnosis, and I call it "suggestive relaxation."

This technique can serve as the foundation for all the mind power exercises in this book, many you've yet to learn. It will be the basis for the synergistic goal-setting exercise in the following chapter. You will learn how to accelerate the programming of your subconscious mind through relaxation and sensory-rich imagery. Any high achiever will agree—salesperson, athlete, performer—that the ability to relax under pressure is critical to success.

Nature's Law

This is as true in your personal life as it is in selling. It's something we all have to be aware of at all times. Nobody is immune.

I can remember one beautiful Saturday afternoon when I was writing a chapter of this book in my study at home. My daughters had a couple of friends visiting for the afternoon, and as four- and seven-year-olds will do, these kids were having a blast. They were under strict instructions "not to bother Daddy while he's working."

Well, I soon realized that's like telling a bee not to make honey. One by one, these four girls took turns coming in to ask me very important questions, like: "Can I have something to drink?" "Can we ride our bikes?" "What are you doing?" I guess it doesn't look much like work to kids to see an adult sitting in front of a computer.

Needless to say, I wasn't getting much work done. I was having difficulty with the chapter I was working on, the kids were bothering me, and I was feeling frustrated and tense. Each time I heard the kids yelling, just having fun, I felt a bit more anxious.

Finally, they all came running down the hall yelling, "Let's play tag, let's play tag, let's play tag!" Reacting, instead of responding, I jumped into the hall, sent the friends home, and banished my daughters to their rooms.

As I returned to my work, I felt terrible. I'd allowed myself to get uptight—and I teach people how to relax! I could control where I worked. I had chosen to work at home because it was a beautiful day and I was hoping I could spend some time with my daughters. Now they were both crying in their rooms because I forgot to practice what I teach. I could have controlled my response if I had been more relaxed.

This is an area everyone needs to address, and, as evidenced by my little transgression above, must be addressed every day. Thus the importance of "suggestive relaxation." This exercise compliments all facets of winning the inner game of selling.

I want to share with you a handful of the comments I've received over the years from salespeople who have mastered the art of suggestive relaxation:

- "I feel more relaxed and confident when under intense pressure in a sales situation."
- "I'm aspirin-free! I no longer suffer from tension headaches at the end of every day."
- "I've got a lot more energy and am a better husband and father as a result . . . I now leave work at work."
- "Little problems no longer bother me, when they used to drive me crazy."
- "It's now easy for me to focus on what I can control. Before I learned how to relax, I was so keyed up I attempted to control everything, and struggled to control anything!"
- "I'm much more goal-focused, as I'm able to visualize my goals before every sales call. I also have more confidence in my presentations."
- Because I feel better about myself, I find it easier to empathize with my customers. I'm a better salesperson."

I could go on, the rewards are endless. Learning how to relax is probably the single most important, and overlooked, ingredient in a healthy lifestyle and a productive sales career. Many people assume they don't have time to practice "suggestive relaxation"; they don't have time to relax. Alas, these are the people who need it most.

Relaxation and communication

The impact relaxation has on your internal channels of communication is truly amazing! Your subconscious mind is much more open to suggestion when you're relaxed. This is why advertisements on television are so powerful. Your conscious mind is relaxed, your imagination is playing along with whatever show you're watching, your subconscious is in a highly responsive mode, and zap, here comes the commercial inferring sexiness, or masculinity, of a particular product.

This power is not to be taken lightly. The Federal Communications Commission was aware of this when they banned cigarette advertising from television, while allowing it to continue in print media. The programming message was too powerful because of the impact on the relaxed subconscious mind. I personally feel the FCC should take a close look at television ads for alcohol. Too many youngsters are being programmed that it's "sexy" to drink.

But we're talking about mega bucks! When I edited this chapter, I happened to be visiting my parents in Westchester, New York, my old childhood stomping grounds. Anyway, as is tradition in my family, following dinner, everyone (mother, father, dog, and me) adjourned into the television room.

We no sooner settled in to watch our beloved New York Mets baseball team, when a sequence of ads sent their programming messages over the airways. They were very poignant and spoke for themselves.

The first was played to upbeat rock music while displaying all sorts of wonderful visuals of success to the theme "all you need is a dollar and a dream." It was an advertisement for the New York lottery! The second was a sexy piece with music, virile men and women running, sweating, hugging, laughing, and drinking beer. A bit more obvious, this was a beer commercial!

How many professional athletes do we read about struggling with alcohol and drugs? I shudder to think about the number of teenagers being influenced. Gambling is no better. It is now being classified as a disease. Pete Rose's gambling addiction only brought recent attention to an ancient problem. So let's promote the lottery?!? What kind of messages are we sending?

Pogo might have been more prophetic than he thought when he said "We've met the enemy and they is us!" Nevertheless. . . .

You can control this power

Relaxation is a natural human function, one we're all capable of enjoying from birth. For those who need to relearn it, all you need is a little practice. It's really quite easy.

I'm referring to a deep state of muscle relaxation, not just "vegging out" in your favorite chair. When you are truly relaxed, your pulse rate and blood pressure decrease, while your respiration becomes slower and more regular. These are very healthy, calming responses. In-

82

vesting 20 to 30 minutes a day relaxing can make a big difference in the quality of your life. You'll be able to incorporate your relaxation minutes into your synergistic goal-setting exercise, which you will learn in detail in the next chapter.

Most people experience difficulty with relaxation techniques—meditation, yoga, self-hypnosis—simply because they do not practice the technique for a long enough period of time. This is the same reason most people never benefit from goal-setting exercises. I've experienced much success in teaching suggestive relaxation because it requires little time, involves goal programming, and little official instruction. It's simple!

Recognizing relaxation and tension

More than 50 years ago, Dr. Edmund Jacobsen devised a method of relaxing that included some 200 exercises. Any wonder why his technique failed to catch on? Yet his work was extremely important. Dr. Jacobsen was a pioneer in the Western world, teaching the relationship between relaxation and tension. He recognized the importance of being able to recognize both states. Sounds simple, but let's give it a try.

Working Partner Exercise:

- Recall an event during the past 24 hours that made you feel uptight—a prospect, client, family, traffic, paperwork, etc.

- Now recall a circumstance, other than sleep or TV, that made you feel extremely relaxed.

It's not unusual for salespeople in my workshops to have an easy time recalling a stressful situation—they often have trouble picking out only one—but there's usually a lot of difficulty relating to relaxation outside of sleep and television.

A little history of relaxation

What Indian yogis and martial arts masters have known for thousands of years has finally taken seed in our high-tech world. Dr. Jacobsen and his associates documented their work with thousands of people suffering from stress-related health problems. I wonder how many of these people were salespeople. Only a handful of occupations involve such high levels of pressure, tension, and stress as does professional selling. It's just that, unless you sell for a living, few people understand the pressures involved.

It was Dr. Jacobsen's belief that by totally relaxing the muscles of the body, one could relax the mind. Yet, as we've discovered through working the electroencephalograph, many people believe they're fully relaxed when they are not. They're simply not aware of hidden tension, and this tension inhibits the communication and programming of the subconscious. Many salespeople fall into this category.

Hey, it's not "cool" to admit being uptight. (It's also not "cool" to earn only a fraction of the income that you're capable of earning.)

Effective Techniques

There are many effective techniques that will enable you to completely relax your muscles and open the communication with your subconscious. Yoga, meditation, prayer, music, guided imagery . . . I've found the best results using therapeutic hypnosis in sending the reprogramming messages for winning the inner game of selling.

In teaching these techniques in my programs, I've taken the powerful programming aspects of therapeutic hypnosis and incorporated them into a nonthreatening version of self-hypnosis, which I call "suggestive relaxation." Much like therapeutic hypnosis, following the relaxation of your muscles, suggestions are given to your subconscious mind. The only difference is that with suggestive relaxation, you control the suggestions.

Through creating mental images in your conscious mind and "suggesting" them as new instructions to your subconscious, you will gain further control over your selling career. Imagine "suggesting" to your subconscious that you earn $150,000 next year!

Before I take you through the five techniques of suggestive relaxation it's important to recognize and understand your relationship with stress. The following profile will help you reflect and, therefore, get more benefit from suggestive relaxation.

PSP: Personal Stress Profile

	Strongly Agree	Mildly Agree	Mildly Disagree	Strongly Disagree
1. I often have headaches.	4	3	2	1
2. I find myself thinking in bed, rather than falling asleep.	4	3	2	1
3. I usually use a good stiff drink to help me relax.	4	3	2	1
4. My heart races when I prospect and present.	4	3	2	1
5. I drive over the speed limit.	4	3	2	1
6. My life seems to be one big rush.	4	3	2	1
7. I am a smoker.	4	3	2	1
8. I do not eat a balanced diet.	4	3	2	1
9. I am overweight.	4	3	2	1
10. I tend to get short tempered when things go wrong.	4	3	2	1

Maximum Score = 40   My Score _____

Score

40 — 36	You are high risk. Practice your control flame and suggestive relaxation exercise in the next chapter.
35 — 29	You better pay attention to your health and stress levels or you'll soon be high risk.
28 — 21	Average. You can do better!
20 — 14	You've got things pretty well in control. Enjoy the exercises.
13 —	You could teach relaxation to Tibetan monks.

Areas For Improvement:

Review the individual items on the Profile and determine specific areas that you need to develop, strengthen, and enhance in your efforts to eliminate procrastination and improve performance. If you:

Circled **4**, you've identified an area to **develop.**

Circled **3**, you've identified an area to **strengthen.**

Circled **2**, you've identified an area to **enhance.**

Select *three areas* to work on between now and your next group meeting. List them below and discuss them with your partner.

#1— _____

#2— _____

#3— _____

Five Techniques in Suggestive Relaxation

1. Breathing
2. Relaxation
3. Imagery
4. Re-programming
5. Control flame

I'll break down each step, provide you with practice exercises and then pull it all together for you. All good things take time, so don't rush through these five critical techniques. What is simple isn't necessarily easy. Most people breathe incorrectly, have trouble relaxing their minds and bodies, have never systematically attempted controlled imagery, and, therefore, are not self-programmers.

Master each technique before attempting to complete the suggestive relaxation exercise. This will save you much frustration, since otherwise you would probably fail to achieve your goals (and I can't allow that). You are about to learn the wonderful art of programming your mind and controlling your life. Go slowly and *enjoy!*

Technique #1: Breathing

Breath is life. We can go weeks without food, days without water, but only minutes without air. Most people take breathing for granted, and as they grow into adulthood, breathe incorrectly. You know the "stomach in, chest out" slogan, and it isn't just used in boot camp. You've probably been conditioned for good posture and poor breathing.

When you stand with your stomach held in and your chest puffed out, most of your air stays high in your chest. Your lungs are, therefore, seldom fully utilized. When you breathe this way during suggestive relaxation, you inhibit your natural physiological relaxation response, which is critical to your programming.

Diaphragmatic breathing is the way nature desired you to breathe, and, therefore, it is easy to learn. The objective is to fill your lungs completely with air, starting with your diaphragm. You can think of this as belly breathing, because your stomach fills with air first and puffs out before your chest does.

A perfect example of belly breathing can be found with a baby. Watch a baby breathe; nature has that little belly rising and falling in perfect rhythm.

I know, you're probably getting impatient with all this talk about breathing. You've made it this far in life and your breathing hasn't seemed to get in your way. Well, let's re-think that statement. If you're carrying around too much tension and stress, if you worry too much, if you get nervous before telephone prospecting, or group presentations, you probably breathe improperly.

Breathing oxygenates your mind and body. Being able to relax, and consequently having more oxygen flowing through your body and to your brain, will boost your confidence in the midst of tense circumstances. You'll find you have more energy to maintain your motivation to keep on prospecting.

As Taisen Deshimaru states in *The Zen Way to Martial Arts* (E. P. Dutton, 1982), "Air contains the energy and the life from the universe which we receive through our lungs and every cell in our bodies, so it is important to know how to breathe."

Working Partner Practice Session:

Step One:
- Lie on the floor in a quiet place where you will not be disturbed for 10 minutes.

- Place your hands on your stomach, directly below the rib cage.
- Take a deep breath.
- Notice how your hands move, if at all. When they move up and down with each breath, you are filling your stomach with air first—you are belly breathing!

Step Two:

- Concentrate on emptying your lungs completely as you breathe.
- Monitor your breathing pattern as you inhale, stomach expanding, upper stomach and chest expanding, and finally filling the upper portion of your lungs.

Step Three:

- Concentrate on your exhalations.
- Empty your lungs completely.
- Do you exhale through your mouth or through your nose?
- Determine whether you are inhaling through your mouth or nose.

Step Four:

- Take a full breath, inhaling through your nose.
- Exhale completely through your mouth.
- Repeat until this pattern feels comfortable.

Step Five:

- Practice Step Four until you can breathe naturally in this pattern, inhaling fully through your nose, and exhaling completely through your mouth.

Welcome to the world of diaphragmatic breathing!

Technique #2: Relaxation

Many people first learned about the importance of relaxation in the 1960's when transcendental meditation took the Western world by storm. TM popularized the belief that the mind controls the body, and by relaxing both the mind and body, one could improve almost every area of life. And, many people spent hundreds of dollars to learn these "special" relaxation techniques.

In 1975, a Harvard physician, Herbert Benson, published the findings of his research in what was to become the best-selling *Relaxation Response* (1975, Morrow). Dr. Benson was able to provide the same benefits as TM for only the price of his book. Relaxation has become a concept that is understood by most, and practiced by few. Let's practice.

Working Partner Practice Exercise:

Step 1:

- Find a quiet spot where you will not be interrupted for 15 minutes.
- Sit in a straight-backed chair with your feet flat on the floor and your hands lying loosely in your lap. (This position is a Westernized yoga-meditative position that will give your posture a similar upright spinal alignment.)

Step 2:

- Take four to five belly breaths.
- Concentrate on each inhalation, exhalation and your relaxation response.

Step 3:

- Clench your jaw firmly, closing it as tightly as you can.
- Keep this clenched position and begin to recognize your muscular involvement.
- Become aware of the sensations in your neck and face.
- Now notice the tension created by clenching your jaw—the tightness in your lower back, stomach, buttocks, legs, and breathing.
- Release your jaw, let it sag and go loose.
- Wiggle your jaw, let it sag, and go loose again.
- Relax it.

Step 4:

- Clench your jaw again and repeat the entire process.
- Be aware of all the sensations associated with this excessive tension and your subsequent relaxation.
- Repeat the clenching exercise from Step 3 with any muscle groups you wish: fist, thigh, etc.
- The objective is to recognize tension vs relaxation.

Step 5:

- Take two belly breaths.
- Close your eyes.
- Picture your feet in your mind, as you concentrate on your breathing. Feel them relax.
- Next, take your mind into your legs; picturing and feeling calves, knees and thighs relaxing.

- Picture your stomach, as it is often a center of stress and tension. Simply feel it getting loose.
- Take your mind into your back, all the way down your spine, letting loose each step of the way. (This is often a storage house of tension.)
- Picture your neck, also a storage place for tension, and let it relax.
- Let a relaxation mask come over your face, loosening every muscle, as if you just released that clenched jaw.

Step 6:

- Practice Step 5 until you feel comfortable with the progressive relaxation.
- Don't rush or become overly concerned with time. You simply want to become accustomed to the suggestive relaxation process when exercised in its entirety.
- Enjoy!

Whatever helps you to relax, whether it is certain music or imagery, by all means, use it. There is no one set way to relax; the practice session above is only a guide.

Technique #3: Imagery

As you really get involved with winning the inner game of selling, you will be doing a lot of work with imagery. In Chapter Three, I involved you in some simple self-image exercises. I asked you to visualize yourself with the successes of doubling your income. I also had you imagine being on the twenty-seventh floor of a high-rise balcony.

Now I want to take you a little further into the power of imagery. There is no "right" way of imaging. Some people are more visual and they can easily picture themselves on the beach. Others are more auditory and might bring to mind various sounds, such as the sound of the ocean. Still others are more kinesthetic and tend to "feel" things as a sensory experience, such as running on the beach, the movement of the waves, or the feeling of lying on the sand.

Even though you probably find one of these easiest, you do have the ability to imagine all of them. For example, imagine lying on the sand at the beach . . . feel the heat from both the sand and the sun. Now, imagine the sound of the ocean . . . the cry of the sea gulls . . . the sound of the wind. Finally, allow your sense of smell and taste to get involved . . . smell and taste the salt water. The more specific your images, the more senses involved, the more powerful the programming.

Imagine the power of being able to conjure up all the sensory details of your future major accomplishments!

Two types of imagery

You can imagine yourself as a spectator, observing yourself on the beach, or in your accomplishment, outside your body. This is like watching yourself on a movie screen.

The second form of imagery is through first hand experience; you're there inside your body living it. This second mode is more difficult, and requires some practice. Most people can easily become "spectators" of their own success movie, so we will begin there. Once you've mastered it, try stepping into your body in your movie.

Working Partner Practice Exercise:

Picture yourself wearing a brand new outfit. Sense all the detail of exactly what you're wearing; money's no object.

Discussion: Were you a spectator or first person? Describe what you saw, the senses that dominated, and how you felt. You can try this exercise with any type of imagery. Remember, there is no perfection.

Technique #4: Re-programming

Finally! You've relaxed your mind and body sufficiently, exercised your imagination with complete sensory details, and now you're ready to program what you want in your subconscious. Here is where you're going to create specific mental images that correspond directly to your long range and intermediate goals—the subject of the next chapter.

You might feel the tendency to skip over this section and move right into synergistic goal-setting. *Don't!* Relaxation and imagery are skills that you need to practice with, if only briefly. The more sensory detail, the more you can guarantee your goals becoming reality. If you can see, feel, touch, taste and hear them, you can take them to the bank!

You are now going to want to feel comfortable with your ability to create the necessary mental images, in sensory detail, of what you want. Naturally, this means you will need to be specific in your goals, but before I have you zeroing in on time-specific, measurable goals, I'd like you to practice imaging big. Like any new skill, this requires a little practice.

Yes, you can do it!

Although each component part of suggestive relaxation is simple, you might experience some frustration along the way. You're exercising an intangible, your mind. Because of this, there's no definitive measuring point to chart your progress, only your monthly commission statement. Don't concern yourself if you can't see all of your goal images, just keep practicing—they will come. Also, there's no such thing as perfection. By simply relaxing and thinking about what you want, you're sending programming signals to your subconscious, even if you can't visualize them.

But I'm certain you can!

Working Partner Exercise:

Picture yourself as a winner:

1. See yourself as a confident, capable salesperson doing a specific activity associated with selling, one that you really want to do well. Picture yourself going through the motions of performing that activity and enjoying it immensely (prospecting, presenting, closing, etc.).

    Write your picture and feelings: _____

    _____

2. Picture yourself completely relaxed and playing with a child.

    Write your picture and feelings: _____

    _____

3. Picture yourself in the den of your dream house.

    Write your picture and feelings: _____

    _____

4. Imagine yourself standing in front of your boss with high self-esteem, full of confidence.

    Write your picture and feelings: _____

    _____

5. Picture yourself shaking hands with your role model, as equals. Write your picture and feelings: _____

_____

_____

Working Partner Re-Programming Practice Session:

- Sit in your straight-backed chair position.
- Take two belly breaths.
- Relax your entire body.
- Create your private peaceful image scene.
- Picture yourself as a high self-esteem achiever.
- Picture yourself as that high self-esteem achiever going through your upcoming day. See yourself interacting with loving care to your family. See yourself performing the activities of a high self-esteem achiever.
- Imagine yourself setting up appointments, making presentations, gathering referrals, following up—all in the image of a true winner.

(Note: These are the same techniques Olympic athletes use to "see themselves through" their best performances. They form a mental image of themselves doing their best; then they go through the motions of doing what they've just daydreamed. It works!)

Technique #5: The Control Flame

Turning tension into sales: One of the reasons so many salespeople lose their dream is that they get overwhelmed with the tension and stress of prospecting, presenting, closing and paperwork. Can you relate? You try to fight these strong feelings with logic, emotions with reason. It's like telling yourself to relax while making a presentation, but your trembling voice doesn't buy it.

The more you try to deny the tension, the more debilitating it becomes, until finally it consumes you. This has been the primary cause of sales "burnout." Here's a wonderful tool that can reverse all this tension.

The control flame

Imagine this scenario: You're about ready to walk into a large account and give a major presentation to four top executives. Normally, you would be feeling tight all over and ready to "get it over with." Instead of fighting these feelings of nervous tension/anxiety with logic, you imagine a flame of a candle; take one full belly breath; visualize releasing those negative feelings as you exhale; and affirm to yourself, "I'm relaxed and confident."

You cannot have two thoughts in your mind at the same time. It's impossible! Many salespeople think they have dozens of thoughts racing through their minds all at once—deadlines, delivery dates, quotas, special orders, discounts—when really their conscious minds are simply working extremely fast, much too fast.

Breathing is your natural physiological relaxation response. By taking a full belly breath, your relaxation response enhances subconscious communication and inner control. This in turn allows you to flush all that negative tension without a struggle, and simultaneously replace it with your own programming affirmation statement. You will learn more about affirmations and self-talk in a later chapter, but for the purpose of your control flame, "I am relaxed and confident!" is a perfect programming statement. This is how it works:

- You recognize negative tension.
- You immediately visualize the flame of a candle.
- You take a full belly breath with the flame still in your mind.
- You concentrate as you exhale, seeing yourself blowing out the flame, and at the same time, blowing out your negative tension.
- You then say to yourself, "I'm relaxed and confident!"

Working Partner Practice Exercise:

Each of you write down a situation where your nerves interfered with your selling performance. Be as specific as possible. Let your partner read this stressful re-creation and you simply use your control flame. Practice with it—it's fun and extremely powerful.

The control flame can be the most versatile mind power technique you will ever encounter. I've used it with compulsive eaters, professional athletes, dancers, students, pilots, you name it. You can effectively deal with any negative thought or emotion by using your control flame with a full belly breath.

In the next chapter, you will be able to apply the power of suggestive relaxation to your daily goal-setting program. Synergistic goal setting is the ultimate mind power tool for turning goals into a mental compulsion.

How do you cope?

Simply follow the instructions given for each of the 14 items listed below. When you have completed all of the items, total your points and place that score in the box provided.*

_____ 1. Give yourself 10 points if you feel that you have a supportive family around you.

_____ 2. Give yourself 10 points if you actively pursue a hobby.

_____ 3. Give yourself 10 points if you belong to some social or activity group that meets once a month (other than your family).

_____ 4. Give yourself 15 points if you are within five pounds of your "ideal" body weight, considering your height and bone structure.

_____ 5. Give yourself 15 points if you practice some form of "deep relaxation" at least three times a week.

_____ 6. Give yourself 5 points for each time you exercise 30 minutes or longer during the course of an average week.

_____ 7. Give yourself 5 points for each nutritionally balanced and wholesome meal you consume during the course of an average day.

_____ 8. Give yourself 5 points if you do something that you really enjoy, that is just for you, during the course of an average week.

_____ 9. Give yourself 10 points if you have some place in your home that you can go in order to relax and/or be by yourself.

_____10. Give yourself 10 points if you practice time management techniques in your daily life.

_____11. Subtract 10 points for each pack of cigarettes you smoke during the course of an average week.

_____12. Subtract 5 points for each evening during the course of an average week that you take any form of medication or chemical substance (including alcohol) to help you sleep.

_____13. Subtract 10 points for each day during the course of an average week that you consume any form of medication or chemical substance (including alcohol) to reduce your anxiety or just calm you down.

_____14. Subtract 5 points for each evening during the course of an average week that you bring work home—work that was meant to be done at your place of employment.

Now calculate your total score and place it in the box below. A "perfect" score would be 115 points. If you scored in the 50-60 range, you probably have an adequate collection of coping strategies for most common sources of stress. However, you should keep in mind that the higher your score, the greater your ability to cope with stress in an effective and healthful manner.

_____ TOTAL SCORE

* This stress assessment test was created by Dr. George S. Everly, Jr., Loyola College of Maryland, 1980.

Wrap-Up

- Relaxation improves subconscious programming.
- Belly breathing is critical to your natural relaxation response.
- Deep muscle relaxation must be practiced.
- Many people are not aware of their level of tension.
- "Suggestive relaxation" is a nonthreatening method of relaxing the conscious mind and body in preparation for programming.
- Your control flame will help you turn tension into sales.
- Practice all five techniques of suggestive relaxation.

IMPORTANT STUFF!

1. List below the stuff you found important in this chapter.

_____

_____

2. What do you want to change? _____

_____

_____

3. When are you going to change it? _____

_____

_____

4. What are you going to enhance?_____

_____

_____

5. How are you going to enhance it? _____

_____

_____

Chapter 8

SYNERGISTIC GOAL SETTING

Now that you've discovered how good it feels to relax completely and tune in to your subconscious mind, let's move ahead to the next step: harmonizing your conscious mind with your subconscious mind, and creating a powerful goal-setting exercise. Let's take a brief look at the different roles.

Conscious Goal Setting Role: It is here where you refine your major accomplishments into measurable, time-specific entities. Once you have consciously determined your goals, you're ready for your daily goal setting exercise. Here, your conscious role is to write out your entire goal statement: long range, intermediate, daily activities. This sends sensory messages to your brain.

Subconscious Goal Setting Role: You should have a good idea of this role by now. It is here you take your consciously written goal statements and spend 10 to 15 minutes using suggestive relaxation to visualize your exact goals in as much detail as possible. You'll be amazed at the increase of sensory detail in your images because of your consciously written statements.

By writing and visualizing what you have written, you will be reprogramming your subconscious mind to accept a new, more successful vision of yourself, a vision that you've carefully sculptured. Through this harmony of mind power, you will bring this vision to reality. You'll learn to change your actions and your habits by changing your attitude about yourself. You will act with more confidence as you strategically improve your performance. This is truly exciting!

Very few people practice a regular goal-setting exercise. And, if they do, it's usually nothing more than reading over an annual goal statement once in awhile. Would you have been able to learn how to read if you had glanced at your school assignments only once in a while? Probably not! Thus it should be no surprise that even salespeople who claim to have goals, rarely achieve them.

You, on the other hand, are going to burn your desires—your goals— deep into your psychic consciousness. Not only will you be spending about 20 minutes every day with your goals, you will be actively exercising both your conscious and subconscious. This is why I can assure you with complete confidence that your goals will become a mental compulsion.

Remember, there is no external competition!

By practicing complete relaxation as you did in the last chapter, you have learned to open up your subconscious mind so it is ready to receive the new signals you want to feed it. Now it's time to get your conscious mind ready to start sending these signals. You'll do this with simple, specific, goal statements—statements that will facilitate pleasant mental images. You will see yourself living the achievements that you've written.

Picture Yourself a Winner

Every salesperson wants to win at the game of selling, but winning means different things to different people. The important thing is to see yourself winning in ways that really matter to you. So create your own images of success, and see yourself experiencing that success in your own selling situation. In previous chapters, I took you through some exercises involving imagery; let's check to see if these success images are coming more naturally.

Working Partner Practice Exercise:

Take each statement separately, read it, take two belly breaths, and visualize what you've read. Spend two to three minutes on each statement.

1. See yourself as a confident, capable person doing something you really want to do. Actually picture yourself going through the motions of doing your job well and enjoying it immensely, or driving a fine automobile you've bought with commissions or bonus checks.

2. Imagine yourself standing before a mirror admiring the look of success.

3. See yourself being commended for your achievements or promoted to the job you wish to have.

Discussion: Are the images coming more naturally? Are you aware of your dominant sensory details? Do you feel like you're forcing the images?

These images should begin to flow more freely into your mind at this point. If you, or your partner, are experiencing any difficulty with these images, relax, you're probably trying too hard. Remember, there is no perfection in imagery—this is not like your television at home. If you feel as though you're really struggling, go back through all five techniques of suggestive relaxation outlined in Chapter 7.

Whatever the goals you determine to set for yourself, you will be seeing yourself accomplishing them every day. The more vivid the mental pictures, the better they will work for you. Why? Because the more detailed your vision, the stronger the signal you're sending to your subconscious mind that you've adopted a new way of seeing yourself.

Now that you've learned to visualize yourself succeeding, let's get on to the concept of synergistic goal setting. This is your key to proactively involving your conscious and subconscious mind, and enlisting these powerful allies in your march toward success.

Synergistic Goal Setting

The word "synergy" describes a situation in which the whole is greater than the sum of all its individual parts. I like to use this word to describe the power that results from combining both the conscious and the subconscious mind in a concerted drive for success. It's a "2 + 2 = 5" sort of thing.

The technique of synergistic goal setting allows you to employ this double-barreled power to become the successful salesperson you want to be. It's a two-step exercise that begins with your conscious mind establishing specific written goals. When you've established these written goals, you then get some pictures that represent these accomplishments, and you're ready for suggestive relaxation. Let's start writing your goals.

Writing your goals

Review the major accomplishments that you established in Chapter 5. Now, you're going to transfer these from abstract "dreams" into time specific, measurable, objectives. This will give you a precise beginning and end.

The structure of synergistic goal setting is this:

Long Range: 3 to 5 years (maximum of 4 sentences)

Intermediate: 1 year (maximum of 4 sentences)

Daily Activities: Your daily routine—fixed behavior that you can totally control

You might want to think of your long-range goal as the second priority of your three major accomplishments. This is simply because the time frame is three to five years into the future. It's a way off, but close enough to be accountable.

Next, look at your intermediate goal as a stepping stone to your long-range goal. Since the time frame is one year away, this can be your top priority major accomplishment.

Only you can determine the priority of your major accomplishments and relegate them into this goal exercise.

This often requires a good deal of thought. Your partner will be very helpful, but the real thought must come from you. You are designing your life in a manner that is becoming a workable reality.

Each step of the process must support the next step. It is like working with an architect on the design of your dream house. Everything is wonderful when you are in the planning stages. But, if attention is not paid to each detail of the final plans so that all of the details come together in the correct order, the end result is more apt to be a lawsuit instead of a warm and exciting home.

Establish both your personal and professional goals

It's helpful to write your goals in two ways. On one page, list the actual results you want to achieve. On another page, list the sensory and emotional components of those results, how it feels, looks, sounds, tastes and smells to reach your goals. In this way, you deal with both your conscious and subconscious mind.

Your conscious mind receives the abstract, written message, while your subconscious mind is programmed to propel you forward through the rich visual picture you've established.

Here's an example: the goal statements of a business client of mine. Of course, yours will be different. But a look at these statements will help you get the idea. First, we'll look at the goal statements themselves, then we'll sample the sensory components of one of these goals.

Written Goal Statements (Conscious Mind)

1. *Long-range* (Three to five years): I am president of XYZ Company earning a salary of $225,000 a year. I have a 50-acre family vacation retreat.

2. *Intermediate* (One Year): I am senior vice-president of marketing earning $85,000. I am a member of ABC Country Club, I live in a 5,000 square foot house, and I spend eight or more quality hours a week with my children.

3. *Daily Activities:*

- I am closing three new accounts.
- I have made 11 telephone prospecting calls resulting in eight appointments.
- I have lunch with my boss, feeling full of confidence and positive energy.
- I attend a 45-minute civic meeting at 4:45 p.m., where I subtly network among potential customers.
- I enjoy a full dinner with my family at 7 p.m.
- I help my wife finalize our family vacation plans.

Now let's take the first written goal, the long-range one, and look at how you would record the sensory components of that goal.

To do so, write the feelings you expect to experience as you accomplish that goal. These are the direct, tangible payoffs you receive from achievement. Simply record what it is like to be there. This will assist you in creating sensory-rich details in suggestive relaxation.

The long-range goal in our example was to be a company president earning $225,000 annually, the owner of a 50-acre family vacation retreat. Here's how to translate that goal into the sensory messages that communicate best to your subconscious mind.

SIGHT: I picture a Thanksgiving reunion at my 50-acre retreat—brothers, sisters, nieces, nephews—all riding horses.

SOUND: I listen as one relative tells another that I am the president of XYZ Company. I hear the joyous laughter of my wife and children as we are horseback riding.

TOUCH: I feel the touch of the horses as my children and I go riding the trails.

SMELL: I savor the earthy aroma of my horse stables.

EMOTIONS: I feel pride in my professional accomplishments and in the relationships I enjoy with my family.

Using your goals each day

To put the magic of synergistic goal setting to work, you need to reinforce daily your determination to meet your goals. I'm going to show you a simple, proven method for doing just that. I call it "The 20-Minute Solution." Use this formula for 20 minutes each day, and you'll be amazed at the results you'll begin to experience.

Gear up

You'll need a datebook or calendar with ample space for writing each day. I like to use one published by Day-Timers, Inc. It's called the "two page per day senior size desk Day-Timers^{tm}, loose-leaf edition with master set." It's well organized and provides plenty of space for your daily entries.

Your daily exercise will combine writing your statements, all in affirmation form, present tense positive (I'll go into more detail on wording affirmations in a later chapter), and practicing suggestive relaxation. Plan to spend about five to seven minutes writing your goal statements and 13 to 15 minutes with suggestive relaxation.

Choose a time for maximum effectiveness

The best time to practice synergistic goal setting is either early in the morning or at night before going to bed. In both cases you will be closer to your subconscious mind, your alpha state, as your conscious mind has either yet to get in full swing, or is beginning to wind down. Go through your 20-minute routine when you feel you will be undisturbed. Let your family know you need some quiet time, or close the door to your office and turn on the answering machine.

I prefer early in the morning. This gives me a real focus for the day. You might be more of an evening person, it really doesn't matter. Whatever time period you choose, make it a permanent fixture in your daily routine. You will find it much easier to develop it into a habit this way.

Try to avoid the time just after eating. Your body is digesting and this tends to interfere with suggestive relaxation.

Write your goals

When writing your goals begin with your long-range ones and work backwards to your daily activities. Again, you should spend between five and seven minutes to write your goals.

Many sales people still wonder why they have to rewrite the same long-range and intermediate goals every day. The answer is simple; if you want your goals to be a compulsion, etched in every part of your being, you have to.

Keep your long-range goals with targets of three to five years, intermediate goals you want to accomplish within a year, and your daily activities as your daily routine. Reduce these to about three to four sentences each, and state them in "present tense positive," as though they're already true. For example, "I am vice president of my division," not "I'd like to be vice president of my division."

Incidentally, you'll find The 20-Minute Solution also works as an excellent time management tool, because it's really self-management. By writing your long-range and intermediate goals, then your daily activities, you'll also be mapping out the steps you need to take to reach those goals, and evaluating yourself each day.

Every day you'll write the same goals in the same order—long-range, intermediate and daily—thus reinforcing these positive images in your subconscious mind. But that's not all. The next step will help you turn those visions into reality.

Relax and imagine your day

Now you're going to implement the technique of suggestive relaxation. Following the precise steps of Technique #4: Re-programming, from Chapter 7, take about 15 minutes, relax and visualize what you've just written.

It's time to put it all together.

Synergistic Goal Setting

1. Write all goal statements:

  • long-range, _____

  _____

  _____

  _____

  • intermediate, and _____

  _____

  _____

  _____

- daily activities. _____

_____

_____

_____

_____

_____

_____

2. Suggestive relaxation:
   - Sit in your straight-backed chair position.
   - Take two belly breaths and close your eyes.
   - Relax your entire body.
   - Create your private peaceful image scene.
   - Picture yourself living your long-range goal, just as you've written it, in as much sensory-rich detail as possible. Include professional, personal, and family images.
   - Imagine yourself living your intermediate goal with the same balance and sensory detail as your long-range goal.
   - See yourself going through your upcoming day carrying out the exact daily activities you've outlined for yourself. Again, use balance and sensory-rich detail.

You should spend about 20 minutes on this exercise. Take as long as you need to complete it in an unhurried manner. Then declare the exercise over and continue your usual activities.

If you practice this exercise faithfully, you'll be amazed at the results that begin to accrue. What you're doing is actively engaging both your conscious and subconscious mind to work for you in creating the life of your choice.

Step by step you'll begin to reach those goals.

Many sales people I've worked with find that within seven or eight months they have to revise their intermediate goals because they've already reached them. That's great! I love to see successful people facing the challenge of upgrading their goals to meet their new capabilities.

What happens if you don't meet your goals? It's possible, though not likely, that you won't quite reach them. But even if you don't, you'll find that you're further along toward being the salesperson you want to be, simply by setting goals and striving to reach them. Try it and I think you'll agree.

Keep practicing your daily suggestive relaxation routine as part of your goal setting once a day. This way your getting two daily benefits; you're teaching yourself how to relax and win, and you are programming your goals into a mental compulsion.

What's important, you've begun to take positive steps, internal steps, toward becoming a winner in the inner game of selling. You may stumble along the way, but stay with it. It's a little like learning how to walk. The first few steps feel awkward, and you stumble over your own feet. But the excitement of opening up a whole new world makes you want to keep trying until you can do it well.

As you keep practicing synergistic goal setting, you'll gain confidence both in the technique and in your ability to do it. You'll discover it gives you a new sense of self-confidence and changes your whole attitude toward yourself and your selling career. The key to making it work is to keep practicing it every day, and that may be your greatest challenge.

Make certain that your working partner agrees to be held accountable, and holds you accountable, for the completion of this daily exercise!

To help you stick with your new program until it becomes second nature, remember these tips:

1. Don't try to reason it all out. The important thing is not how it works, but that it does work for you.

2. Don't try to evaluate the technique or analyze your success with it. Just do it!

3. Don't worry about the time. Some people can do their routine in 10 minutes, while others require 30 or more. Set your own pace and take time to make the exercise enjoyable.

4. Don't look for shortcuts. There aren't any. The system has been scientifically developed and carefully tested with thousands of people.

5. Follow the instructions precisely, and accept the fact that there is a good reason for each of them. For example, we suggest you always sit up in a straight chair because it's the only way your mind can get the exercise it needs. If you try the routine lying down, the bed does the relaxing for you, and you may easily fall asleep without gaining any benefit from your work.

6. Don't discuss your synergistic goal setting with anyone outside your immediate support team, your working partner and, possibly, your

spouse. It's not a big secret. It's just that goals work much better when they are very personal and private. There will be plenty of time to brag about the results later.

7. Don't look for quick results. You didn't develop into what you are overnight, and you won't be able to be a high self-esteem achiever by tomorrow. It takes about three weeks to break an old pattern, and about six weeks to establish a new one. Keep putting in the time, and you'll reap plentiful rewards, a whole new way of living and selling.

8. Don't struggle with your negative self-concept. Relax and trust the suggestive relaxation system, even if you don't always feel like you're making a lot of progress. You can do it, and it will work for you.

9. Try to build suggestive relaxation into your daily routine so that it becomes a normal part of everyday life—belly breathing, control flame, and muscle relaxation.

10. Stay with it! Real progress comes slowly, but produces lasting results. Give yourself some time.

Congratulations! You've passed another milestone on the path of becoming a consistent winner at the inner game of selling. Simple, isn't it? It's just a matter of doing many of the same things you've done in some form all your life, but doing them in a structured way. In fact, it's so simple you may wonder how it can work. Believe me, I've watched it work with thousands of people, and I can assure you it will work for you.

Don't stop until you reach your destination—winning the inner game of selling. And don't worry about the outer game of selling. When you start consistently winning the inner game, you'll see a dramatic improvement in your sales performance. You'll become a top professional who can sell anything, and you'll love it.

Wrap-up

- You involve your conscious mind when you write your goals.
- Your subconscious mind is activated by using suggestive relaxation and visualizing your goals—just as you've written them.
- A synergy is where the whole is greater than the sum of all its individual parts.
- Long-range goals represent your dream (three–five years), intermediate goals are the stepping stones (one year), and your daily activities are your "to-do list."

- Goals become more real when you experience the feelings that accompany their accomplishment.
- Practice synergistic goal setting daily! Your goals will then become a mental compulsion.
- Hold your working partner, and yourself, accountable for investing 20 minutes daily to synergistic goal setting.

IMPORTANT STUFF!

1. List below the stuff you found important in this chapter.

    _____

    _____

2. What do you want to change? _____

    _____

    _____

3. When are you going to change it? _____

    _____

    _____

4. What are you going to enhance?_____

    _____

    _____

5. How are you going to enhance it? _____

    _____

    _____

Chapter 9

MEET YOUR GREATEST SALES TOOL

Your *mind* is your greatest sales tool. In fact, this God-given intangible is virtually limitless in its potential! Yet, even though the mind has been studied throughout recorded history it is seldom, if ever, fully utilized. To grasp the law of the mind, and persistently apply it to your life, is to gain mastery of a power that defies imagination.

Every triumph made by man has been the result of mental effort. Breakthroughs in the fine arts, high technology, exploration, medicine, were all the direct result of a disciplined application of mind power.

Long ago, it was said that the greatest sin of mankind was one of omission, neglecting the potential of the mind. Unfortunately, most people have never been taught how to use this great asset.

Nondenominational power

To capitalize on your mind power, you must have faith. True faith, the ability to believe without proof, is nondenominational. And, there's a lot more to religion than going to church or synagogue every week.

I know people who are extremely faithful in their belief in God; they're loving, caring, generous people who do not attend church on a regular basis. I also know people, as I'm sure you do, who attend services every week and are miserable, bitter and consumed with worry and fear. Maybe they're waiting for divine intervention, but as far as I'm concerned they've yet to recognize their true spiritual powers. God helps those who help themselves. Right?

I'm convinced that everyone needs a personal relationship with God. This is nondenominational! It's my opinion that you will only reach your potential as a human being by embellishing this relationship. You must be able to believe without proof. Accepting the fact, there's a greater power—a force, if you choose—that is readily available to all who ask.

I am not selling religion, I'm establishing the timeless power of faith. This is a must for you and your partner—it's a must for ongoing personal and professional growth. Whether you attend services regularly, worship on a personal level with your family, or commune in private with the elemental good, makes no difference to maximizing your potential. The true measure of your spiritual being is your character, your goodness, and your willingness to make full use of the forces given to you at birth.

Is faith necessary?

Is faith really necessary? Does the ability to believe bear a direct correlation to success? Think about the following example from my files. I was giving the fifth and final session of an "Inner Selling Achievement Group" for a large insurance company. The group was composed of ten managers, and in the preceding sessions each member had established personal and professional goals. For accountability purposes, I requested the professional goals be supported by real dollar figures.

During the course of the sessions I had taught all the principles of winning the inner game of selling . . . everybody had a working partner . . . reading assignments . . . goal setting exercises . . . everything that you have learned about. Each member had established their daily specific activities.

As we began the final session it was apparent that Albert Barr was troubled. He had struggled with his activities, he always seemed to be in a rush to leave each session, never had time for the take-home exercises, and his input was usually negative. He loved to complain about the company's management team. Because he was the senior member of the group, the other members simply let Albert be Albert— for a while.

Albert's moment of truth

Rather than asking him to leave the group because he wasn't contributing, his peers allowed him to continue with the sessions, probably out of respect more than anything else. Anyway . . .

The moment of truth was approaching and Albert was visibly uncomfortable. Everyone was to report their performance figures, numbers each had set for themselves in dollars, over the past 120 days. Apparently Albert couldn't stand the tension, so he started by saying "I've been busting my butt for this program. I've given up valuable time to this program and I can't see that it's doing me any good."

His working partner, Darryl, quickly jumped in. "Could it be, Albert, that you really haven't learned anything about your mind from these sessions? You never completed the growth exercises, you seemed to go through the motions relating to the message Matt is teaching with the inner game. I don't think you really believe in the power of the mind. Why don't you tell the group your performance dollars over the past four months."

You can't imagine how thankful I was to Darryl. He was holding his working partner accountable to perform. There were going to be no last minute excuses. Albert hesitated for a moment and then wrote his production figures on the board. They were embarrassingly low! And, the rest of the group had significantly improved their income. Everybody who had faith was writing more business. Albert, who did not believe, wasn't!

The group voted to extend my contract, but asked Albert not to participate. Albert was crushed! It wasn't so much being asked to leave, but that he lost face in front of his peers. The years of influence he held over these managers had vanished in only 120 days. Albert refused to believe, while his peers learned how to tap into the magic of their minds. They weren't about to be influenced by someone who refused to believe.

Make certain your working partner buys in to all the mental exercises! Accessing the power of your subconscious mind is a must!

Going through the motions, like Albert, will only further damage your self-esteem. You and your working partner must have faith in the powers of the mind.

David and Goliath

A salesman friend of mine has a plaque on his wall proclaiming one of the gems of wisdom about the game of selling. It says, "David killed Goliath with the jawbone of an ass. Most sales are lost with the same vehicle."

Yet, if you ask most salespeople what's their most powerful tool for selling, they'll say, "My ability to talk." Other common answers are "my personality," "product knowledge," or "a good sales pitch." This is the same external game of selling that Albert prided himself on understanding.

But are these truly the keys to sales success? Of course not! The IQ/SQ exercise you completed with your working partner in Chapter 4 indicates most salespeople don't really consider these qualities critical to success. Let's take a look at some of the reasons why Albert couldn't keep up with his peers.

Lessons of a Zen master

An ancient story illustrates Albert's saga very clearly. The story tells of a professor of Zen Buddhism who seeks counsel with a Zen Master to learn the finer points of meditation. As soon as the master invites the professor in for tea, the professor begins talking about Zen philosophy, attempting to impress the master with his knowledge.

The master listens patiently for a good while and then asks the professor if he would like some tea. The professor agrees, as he continues talking, and the master began to pour tea into the professor's cup. The cup fills up, yet the master continues to pour, spilling tea all over the table and the professor. Startled, the professor asks what the master is doing. The master calmly replied that his cup was so full, there was no room for the tea.

How often do you run into salespeople who, like the professor, are so full of their own knowledge that there is little room for learning? Have you ever been guilty of this? Poor Albert will be incapable of any type of growth until he lets go of some of his existing knowledge. Preconceived notions, unsubstantiated with first hand experience, are impediments to learning. You are making a commitment with yourself and your partner to learn continually, as you enjoy your success journey on earth.

You're about to use your mind more completely than ever before. Now's the time to flush out any preconceived notions and open your mind wide!

Think for a moment about the last time you struggled with a decision over whether or not to make a cold call. You knew that the only way you could make a sale was to call on that prospect, but you felt a strong and compelling force inside you that seemed to take control of your will, dominate your thoughts, and wreak havoc with your emotions. You simply did not want to knock on that door, or pick up the phone and call that prospect.

That kind of struggle can be depressing. It can make you dislike yourself and destroy any semblance of self-confidence you may have. Yet studies show it is one of the most common struggles salespeople go through.

Recently, I received hundreds of letters in response to the column I write for *Insurance Sales* magazine, titled "Better Prospecting & Selling." Wanting to make this a column of the agents and for the agents, I asked for write-in questions. Not only was my office overwhelmed with mail, many of the letters had a common theme. The following is a fairly good representation:

Dear Matt:

I know I am not at my full potential. I am very knowledgable, fully understand the sales process but cannot make myself work everyday. When I work, I work harder than anyone but I cannot stay at that level. When I don't make calls, I get down on myself and question my abilities. When I have activity, I feel great. How can I motivate myself to be consistent?

Sincerely yours,

A Frustrated Life Agent

The real message in this letter concerned the fine line between confidence and depression, action and inaction, high self-esteem and low self-esteem, and success and failure. This epitomizes the professional sales game.

But the wonders of the mind are available to all who are interested. By simply understanding how the mind works and following the basic exercises in this book, the frustrated agent of the letter above, Albert, or any other salesperson, can develop into a true high achiever.

But what if . . . . ?

But what if this life agent could reverse all that negative mental and emotional energy and make it work for him, instead of letting it tear him apart? What if he could turn things around so that he was compelled just as strongly to make that cold call every day, day after day?

What if you could do the same? What if you could change your feelings about selling so completely that you simply could not wait until it was time to talk to a new prospect?

I'll tell you some good news. You can do all these things and more. You can learn to redirect all the power of your mind to exert just as much pressure in the direction of becoming successful as it now exerts in the direction of running from sales opportunities. It can become as natural for you to sell as it now is for you to retreat from selling situations.

Your mind will become your most powerful ally as you understand, first, how it operates, and second, how it can best operate for you. To begin this understanding, let's look at some basic information about how your mind works.

Controlling your gentle giant

Your mind is like a great giant with almost limitless power, who wants to serve your every need. The mind is what makes us human. It elevates us above the rest of the life on this planet. This powerful resource provides our ability to think, to reason, to create, to dream—to be the dominant force on the earth.

Aristotle considered the mind as something related to the heart. Plato thought it to be aligned to the brain. In 1981, Dr. Roger Sperry, a psychobiologist at California Institute of Technology won a Nobel Prize for Physiology and Medicine for his work on the functioning of the two hemispheres of the brain. This has been referred to as "split brain" research.

Dr. Sperry was able to prove that we actually have a left and a right brain that are connected by a communications network called the corpus collosum. His research revealed that each hemisphere was responsible for various activities: analytical—thinking functions with the left, and creativity—intuition with the right.

The infinite power of your mind

The fact is, much like the relationship between the heart and soul, the brain and mind are inextricably linked. Research scientists are comfortable studying the heart and brain, as these are tangible organs that can be seen and touched in their laboratories. They know the average brain weighs a little over three pounds and has more storage capacity than the largest computer ever built.

116

It's been said that the typical human brain can store up to two quintillion bits of information. In numbers, that's 2,000,000,000,000,000,000. Soviet brain specialist, Ivan Yefremov, says the average human being has enough brain power to master 40 foreign languages, commit any given set of encyclopedias to memory, and successfully complete the required courses of a dozen universities.

All of this is wonderful, but nobody has ever seen a mind. With all of this documented brain power, there still is difficulty even defining the mind. Yet there is universal agreement that even the most brilliant human beings only use a fraction of their mental powers.

Consider your spiritual consciousness. Some people refer to this power as psychic energy, others call it intuition. Regardless, the label you affix is not important. How you refer to the powers of your mind, to what you attribute their origin, is secondary to your belief in their existence.

"OK, OK enough already," you're thinking. "All I'm interested in is learning how to make more money." Right?! Hold your horses, Albert, and let me share two illustrations that will demonstrate how insidious, yet powerful, the forces of your mind are in your life.

Positive Forces: Picture yourself getting ready for a seven-day cruise that you won in a sales contest. You are excited! Your plane is leaving at 7 a.m. and you're up late with last minute packing and getting the house ready. You're anxious about getting up in time so you set two alarm clocks to wake you at 5 a.m.

You drift off to sleep with visions of the cruise in your mind and knowing you must get up at 5 a.m. A miracle occurs! You wake up at 4:59 a.m. before the alarms! Has something like this ever happened to you?

Negative Forces: Imagine getting ready to call on a major prospect. Your boss is on your case because there's a lot of potential business at stake, you've been treated very rough in your past attempts to get an appointment, and now you know you've got to call on this company in person in the morning. You go to bed early, worrying about the imagined ego-bruising day you're about to encounter. You spend a restless night in bed, oversleep, get to the office late, and then talk yourself out of making the call. Can you relate?

Mind power is either constructive or destructive. There's no middle ground. With very little effort you can program your subconscious to awaken you in the morning, or to develop a serious problem with call reluctance. In either case, mind power was involved without any conscious intention. Just imagine the power you've got at your disposal when harnessed and directed toward personal and professional goals!

Wrap-Up

- Your mind is your greatest tool!
- The greatest sin of mankind is one of omission; neglecting the mind.
- Faith is nondenominational.
- Mind power is nondenominational.
- Achievers believe without proof.
- Lessons of a Zen Master; is your cup too full to learn?
- The mind elevates us above all other creatures on the planet.
- Your mind power is either constructive or destructive; the choice is yours!

IMPORTANT STUFF!

1. List below the stuff you found important in this chapter.

_____

_____

2. What do you want to change? _____

_____

_____

3. When are you going to change it? _____

_____

_____

4. What are you going to enhance?_____

_____

_____

5. How are you going to enhance it? _____

_____

_____

Chapter 10

THE PROGRAMMING POWERS OF THE MIND

I've flooded this chapter with quotes for a very specific reason. As you read them, notice that they all portray the same message, even though they are taken from entirely different cultures and times. My point is that the message of the inner game is universal and timeless. Now is your time!

Tis the mind that makes the body rich.—Shakespeare

Most everyone has heard about the conscious mind and the subconscious mind. The subconscious is considered by experts to be 90 percent or more of our latent mental power. It is like a huge untapped reservoir. While our conscious mind is considered to be the much smaller part of our mind, less than 10 percent.

The exact percentages are not important; it's your understanding of the specific roles each plays that I'm concerned with.

The mind is everything; what you think, you become.—
Gautama Buddha

For the purposes of this writing, let me break down the definitions as they will be used.

The Conscious Mind

Here lies our thinking mind, our ability to rationalize and reason. Although it is considered to be less than 10 percent of our mental power, in many ways it is the key to all our power. It was your conscious thoughts that programmed you to wake up at 4:59 a.m. to catch a flight to your cruise. Your enthusiasm and excitement dominated your consciousness, and the programming was natural.

Conversely, your conscious thoughts programmed you to develop a problem with call reluctance. Because worry and anxiety dominated the consciousness, programming call reluctance was also very natural.

This is a basic law of the mind. If you think it long enough, you will live it. Dwell on a thought, good or bad, and it becomes programmed into your subconscious mind. Your behavior then becomes automatic. Thus, the power of synergistic goal setting.

As children, we are taught by our parents and teachers to think. In essence, we are taught how to use only our conscious mind without any consideration to our subconscious. Much emphasis is placed on thinking. We are taught to remember, to be logical, pay attention, and are rewarded for mastery of such conscious skills.

Unfortunately, the skills that enable a person to get good grades in the classroom are not always transferable to the real world. This is why many "A" students never achieve what one might expect, and many "average" or even "poor" students go far beyond expectations. Most salespeople are aware of this deep down inside, evidenced by the feedback from my IQ/SQ survey.

Our youth

He who thinks far, goes far.—Belgian proverb

What a shame it is to watch graduates from our universities, proficient in sciences, computers, languages, music, mathematics, being held back because of a poor working knowledge of the mind. College graduates, full of theories and knowledge, frequently suffer from low self-esteem and a poor self-image. They have no understanding of how to program success habits, build self-esteem and confidence, or how to believe without proof.

Children must be taught to expect success. Parents and teachers need to teach youngsters to believe in themselves, that they are born to achieve. The problem, as I see it, is that parents and teachers cannot teach what they don't understand. There's an anonymous quote that dates back to the late nineteenth century that says, "We know more about breeding high grades of cattle, than we do about developing high quality adults." Doesn't appear that much has changed by the end of the twentieth century!

There is no question that children who possess a working understanding of their mind will be much more likely to develop into high quality adults who can control their destiny.

Programming thoughts

It's important to understand that every conscious thought sends a programming message to your subconscious mind. Thoughts that are repeated over and over determine our automatic behavior. They become the recorded tapes that play in our heads. This is the foundation for all habits, good and bad.

The reason many insomniacs toss and turn all night is that they bombard their subconscious with thoughts of their struggle with sleep throughout the day. This anticipatory anxiety, to use a term coined by Austrian psychiatrist Victor Frankel, is simply a dysfunctional use of the conscious mind. It frequently becomes a bad habit.

The thoughts of his heart, these are the wealth of a man.
—Burmese proverb

Conscious thoughts and call reluctance

One of the most damaging occurrences for a salesperson, or any person for that matter, is to become dysfunctional with conscious thoughts. Just about every type of fear you can imagine begins with a repeated thought. Fear of failure, fear of success, call reluctance, and low self-esteem are all programs created by conscious thoughts.

Since most people can only relate to their immediate conscious thoughts, their dysfunctional nature is difficult to detect. This makes sense when you consider that the very thoughts that are dwelled on and need flushing, are your primary communicating link to yourself, and the world around you. Unfortunately, too often they don't provide accurate information.

Try to relate to this scenario: Doug is a life insurance agent who doesn't like prospecting. His connections in the community are so strong that he was able to make rookie of the year by simply getting the word out that he was in the life insurance business. While he was writing all this business, no phone activity was taking place.

Doug, through dwelling on his dislike of prospecting, reached the point where he detested the phone. By the end of the first year, after winning all the company awards and using up all his connections, Doug had developed a phobic case of call reluctance.

Doug's story is an actual case of an agent with a company I was working with at the time. At his manager's request, he became a private client of mine. I'd like to say Doug is making 25 prospecting calls a day. He's not, but at least he's now calling his referrals and averaging about ten calls every day. By understanding how to use the power of his conscious thoughts, Doug has been able to begin to correct a potentially career-threatening problem.

No longer does Doug talk about how much he hates prospecting. Doug now talks about how much he loves the opportunities in his business. He's now in control of the programming in his mind. He also is devoting 20 minutes a day to synergistic goal setting.

He can who believes he can.—Latin proverb

Here's another little exercise to try and then discuss with your working partner:

Working Partner Exercise:

What will you purchase when you double your income in 12 months? A new car, a boat, a house . . .? Write it down on paper, then close your eyes and, through the power of imagination, visualize this purchase already in your possession. Mentally see yourself, feel yourself, sense yourself experiencing the pleasures of this new purchase. See yourself one year from today, as if it were now, living your dream.

Working partner discussion: What did you purchase? How clear was your visualization? What were the details of your visualization? How did the exercise make you feel? Were you able to improve the clarity of the sensory detail?

This was really two exercises in one. When you determined your purchase of one year from now, you exercised your conscious mind by thinking about that particular item. But when you imagined the purchase as already coming true, you exercised the power of your subconscious mind by using visualization skills. This is the crux of mind power—the ability to use your conscious and subconscious minds in harmony to produce desired results. Sound like synergistic goal setting? It is, just a mini-version.

Labels

At first, poor Doug would have trouble with the exercise above because he has labeled himself as a call reluctant salesperson. He'd begin visualizing his doubled income and start feeling tension from the subconscious. Why? His program is for call reluctance. Doug needed to change his programming. Initially, he used his 20-minute goal-setting time to work on his personal self-image. Once Doug began to see himself as a more capable person, free of the labels, he was able to visualize his successes in advance.

Many people suffer from negative labeling done by others. Have you ever been labeled by a parent or teacher in a way that it affected your performance? Maybe a physical education teacher called you a wimp over and over, or a math teacher called you stupid, or your father always referred to you as lazy. Has something like this ever happened to you?

I can recall my high school calculus teacher calling me an "idiot" in front the entire class. I flunked calculus. This negative labeling is criminal! It is usually the beginning of some type of self-limiting behavior, programmed in the subconscious.

> All that we are is the result of what we have thought; it is founded on our thoughts; it is made up of our thoughts.
> —Buddhism proverb

Learning to work smart—not hard

Understanding how your conscious mind programs your automatic behavior will enable you to work smart. As I've already mentioned, but it's worth repeating, too many people wear themselves out working hard. The problem is that they're programmed wrong and, therefore, aren't working smart. A key point to accessing mind power is learning to use the power of positive programming, rather than the power of positive thinking.

Positive thoughts on top of a negative program only create tension. Since all tension seeks resolution, the tendency is to revert back to your pre-existing automatic negative program. You will be avoiding this trap with the exercises in the following chapter.

As I've already mentioned, the conscious mind tends to be familiar to most people. If the brain is the world's most powerful computer, the conscious mind is the most valuable computer programmer. We receive information, we reason, and we act. Though the conscious mind accounts for only five to ten percent of our mind power, it's of critical importance. It carries out what we refer to as "thinking." Herein lies one of its greatest problems. Our thoughts are what determine our automatic behavior because they program our subconscious minds.

Doug couldn't help developing call reluctance, when he continually thought about how much he hated prospecting.

For the purpose of winning the inner game of selling, remember that the conscious mind is your center of reason. It makes choices. For instance, you choose where you work, your home, and your spouse. Every decision is made with your conscious mind. Where people encounter problems with this power to reason is in rationalizing negative behavior. Too many people make too many excuses!

Your conscious mind is your *doing* state. You have direct control over this component. I want you to consider this cycle (what I call the achievement cycle):

DOING: Walking, talking, phoning . . . these are acts—do's— which involve consciously controlled, voluntary movement of some part of the body. You have complete control over this component. This is the action phase of the cycle and it dictates the remaining components. Reading this book is an act. Your working partnership is an act. Synergistic goal setting is an act.

Action cures fear!

Action builds confidence and self-esteem!

Action gets results!

THINKING: You have voluntary and involuntary thoughts. As the case with Doug, he developed a habit of focusing on self-limiting thoughts. They became involuntary. But by changing how he acted, by doing, he was able to get control over those involuntary thoughts that were once programmed in his subconscious mind.

But to change, you frequently must act in a manner that is somewhat uncomfortable. This is good! And by controlling those involuntary thoughts of your subconscious, you begin to have an impact on your feelings.

FEELING: One of the many blessings we have as human beings is a wide range of feelings—anger, joy, excitement, motivation, laziness. For many people this blessing turns into a curse. So much of your total behavior is probably determined by how you feel. If you feel good, you act and make that prospecting call. If you don't, oh well?

Much like your involuntary thoughts, your feelings are deep-seated within you. They are involuntary, as your subconscious mind is simply playing the program that has been recorded. You don't want to feel down. You are envious of a friend of yours who's always in a good mood, but it's almost as though it's out of your control—you're down. Has this ever happened to you?

Well-planned *doing* will enable you to change all of your subconscious programming, that involuntary self-limiting thinking, that feeling of depression that has so often put a halt to the best intentions. So, let's take a closer look at your subconscious.

Your subconscious mind

Your subconscious mind is the center of your emotions, your habits, and all of your involuntary behavior. It is your creative mind. If you were to consider your conscious mind to be rational, your subconscious operates on an irrational level. You think with your conscious mind, and thoughts that are repeated enough sink into, and actually program, your subconscious mind.

What makes your subconscious mind so irrational is that it cannot distinguish between fact or fiction. It accepts any repeated thought as fact. Therefore, this omnipotent force, considered to be well over 90 percent of your mind power, is actually a hostage to your conscious thoughts. Sounds pretty irrational, doesn't it?

Yes and no. This only creates trouble when your conscious mind is not sending healthy messages to your subconscious. Let's take call reluctance, for example. This malady is often considered the culprit for failure in professional selling. Yet, there is no rational basis to the reluctance. I can't ever recall a salesperson getting assaulted, kidnapped or threatened as a result of making a prospecting telephone call. In fact, Doug was the leading rookie in his company. Yet how many salespeople do you know who struggle with this? It's irrational and it's a function of subconscious programming. Have you ever experienced anything like this?

Your subconscious garden

Before the advent of computers, the subconscious mind was often referred to as a garden. If you have ever planted a garden, you know the soil does not discriminate between the seeds you plant and weeds. Your soil accepts any seed, good or bad. In fact, if you're not careful with your garden, weeds tend to dominate. You can view the planting as doing and consider your thoughts in terms of the seeds planted in the garden, your subconscious mind.

Like your garden, your subconscious accepts all seeds as equal. And if you're not careful, negative programming thoughts might tend to dominate.

The most important point to remember about your subconscious mind is that it is incapable of determining whether your thoughts are true or false, good or bad, healthy or unhealthy. Rather, it responds to whatever thoughts are repeated over and over and over. These are the seeds that get planted. This is the programming you are going to learn how to master. The importance of being proactive on *doing* what is within your control can't be stressed strongly enough!

The power of suggestion

Human beings are extremely vulnerable to the power of suggestion, from ourselves and others. Why? Because our subconscious mind simply accepts all sensory input, and suggestions are certainly sensory input. If the sensory input happens to coincide with previous programming, the impact can be immediate.

The negative feeling k.o.

You've probably witnessed this classic example of the power of suggestion in prospecting. You're getting yourself psyched up to call a major-dollar prospect. This prospect is an intimidator and has never done business with your company. But you think you've got an angle and you're going to persevere. Just prior to picking up the telephone, you discuss it with another salesperson in your company and you are told: "Don't waste your time with XYZ company. They'll string you along for months and never buy anything from you. Believe me, I've been there!"

You then feel a knot developing in your stomach and instead of making that phone call, you get some coffee and busy yourself with paperwork.

Because you are feeling-driven, and your feelings have been negatively programmed in your subconscious, the innocent, albeit career threatening, suggestion by your counterpart was congruent with your own feelings. You've allowed yourself to be programmed full of anxieties and fears toward prospecting. Your conscious mind, therefore, accepts this suggestion, and you cannot possibly make that call. You fail to do the most important component of change, the component you're supposed to be in total control of, *doing*. You've knocked yourself out of the game.

The positive feeling home run

Let's take the top salesperson with your company. He is about to make the same high-powered prospecting call. He is getting psyched for the telephone conversation. The situation is the same, your company has never done business with XYZ company. An associate walks in just before the top salesperson is about to dial, notices the company's name and number by the phone, and says, "You're going to waste your time with those people. They've never bought from us and they always string people along."

This person acts! The prospecting call is made by the top salesperson—a home run. That single negative suggestion was no match for the pre-existing subconscious programming to act on his beliefs. Instead of being feeling-driven, fueling fears, this suggestion did not compute. It simply wasn't congruent with the subconscious programming that associated prospecting with making money.

No suggestion can be acted upon by the subconscious that is against the will of the conscious mind. Your conscious mind is your filtering device. Its job is to reject all inappropriate suggestions because the subconscious cannot. The conscious mind of the successful salesperson will always reject any negative message associated with prospecting.

The average salesperson who's struggling to get by will allow the negative message in because it validates previous programming. Therefore, many people suffer from call reluctance simply because of this mixed-up relationship between the conscious and subconscious mind.

No one deceives us more than our own thoughts.
—Silesian proverbs

The reticular activating system

What helps your conscious mind filter information that you receive is a net-like group of cells at the base of your brain. This device is called the reticular activating system. It screens the thousands of messages that pass through the brain daily, sending along to the cerebral cortex those worthy of response.

For example, your brain has the capability of being aware of every sensory exposure of the body, from sunlight on the face to the feeling of food being digested through the intestines. Obviously, a keen awareness of all these sensory messages would simply be too much. The reticular activating system screens out all messages except those that are of two types: messages of value and messages that are threatening.

A message of value

Consider the process of buying a new automobile. You research the market thoroughly and heighten your awareness of information relating to the cars in your price range. You finally settle on one particular model, and as soon as you purchase the car, it becomes something "of value" to you. As a result, even though you own the car and your search is over, you notice every similar model car on the road.

Your reticular activating system works in the same fashion with your goal thoughts. This is why I will ask you to involve yourself with written, spoken, and recorded goal messages. Your reticular activating system will automatically work for you.

A threatening message

Another example is a mother who can sleep through any early morning alarm clock. When her children are infants, sleeping in another bedroom, the slightest cry will wake her out of a dead sleep. Her reticular activating system was allowing that information to enter as a threat.

How easily threats can be programmed

I was listening to Lou Tice give his description of the reticular activating system. He used an analogy of a rock in the middle of the road. Focus on the rock, and you'll hit it. This reminded me of an embarrassing moment with my daughter Heidi. She was anxious to learn how to ride a bicycle without training wheels. So one Sunday afternoon I took the training wheels off her bike and we went out to our side street for a lesson.

Heidi was excited as I sat her on the bike, but then I noticed a small pot hole in the road. Making the mistake of focusing on the pot hole, I became concerned that Heidi might ride into it, so I told her to watch out for the pot hole. I told her "Whatever you do, don't ride into the pothole because you could get hurt." Well, guess what? She rode directly into the pothole, almost as if it had a magnetic attraction. I had inadvertently made it into a threat and activated her reticular system.

Have you inadvertently turned the idea of being rejected into a threat? If you do so, you're probably allowing information, no matter how remote, to filter into your subconscious, information that could be perceived as harmful in relation to rejection.

It's fairly simple to determine what kind of an impact your daily goal setting exercise is going to have on your reticular activating system. These messages, perceived as value, will always be allowed entrance. Threatening messages will take a definite back seat, which is where they need to be for high achievement. Don't worry, you'll be notified in case of an emergency.

For many salespeople, fears of rejection and anxieties toward prospecting mean that the reticular activating system floods the brain with threatening information, leaving little room for positive messages of value. This in turn directly affects the thoughts the conscious mind repeats and a vicious negative cycle is developed. You are in the process of reversing this cycle. In the next chapter, I will take you, step by step, through a process that will give you complete control over your programming cycle.

As I repeat King Solomon's wisdom: "As a man thinketh in his heart, so is he," think good thoughts, look on the bright side of life, look for the good in people, and good things will follow in your life. Whatever your conscious mind believes, your subconscious mind will act upon.

> Mind is the great lever of all things; human thought is the process by which human ends are ultimately answered.
>
> —Daniel Webster

Wrap-Up

- Your conscious mind is your rational thinking mind.
- Your subconscious mind is your irrational mind that cannot distinguish between fact or fiction, good or bad, right or wrong.
- Your conscious mind, although less than 10 percent of your mind power, programs your subconscious mind.
- Your subconscious mind is like a gentle giant, over 90 percent of your mind power, center of your creativity, imagination, and all automatic behavior—habits.
- Doing — Thinking — Feeling: Be a DOER!
- You are extremely suggestible as long as suggestions are congruent with your subconscious programming.
- Your reticular activating system allows only valuable or threatening information to enter your mind.

- Your mind works either constructively or destructively.
- Labels are frequently self-limiting.
- The crux of mind power is conscious and subconscious harmony.
- The mind is easily programmed; beware of negativity from others.
- The inner game, the message of the mind, is universal and timeless.

IMPORTANT STUFF!

1. List below the stuff you found important in this chapter.

_____

_____

2. What do you want to change? _____

_____

_____

3. When are you going to change it? _____

_____

_____

4. What are you going to enhance?_____

_____

_____

5. How are you going to enhance it? _____

_____

_____

Chapter 11

BUILDING A WINNING ATTITUDE

I want you to get together with your partner to analyze your attitude.

Nothing is more critical to your ability to capitalize on your God-given resources than your attitude. I have witnessed salespeople with attitudes that were holding them back to such a degree that, not only did they fail to realize it, they would get hostile at any outside attempts to address the problem. Much like the prototypical ostrich burying its head in the sand, these salespeople refused to accept the fact that their attitude was their biggest enemy.

This reminds me of the story about a teacher who offered his students a prize of $500 for the best thought. The prize was awarded to a student who gave the following thought: "Men grumble because God put thorns with roses; wouldn't it be better to thank God that he put roses with thorns?" That statement is worth far more than five hundred dollars to anyone who fully grasps its depth.

Although this recognition might appear easy on the written page, I can assure you from personal experience that it's not. I was a senior in undergraduate school when I had an attitude realization. Looking back, it's easy to see how I was much more insecure than I wanted anyone to know. To cover up this feeling of inferiority, I spent countless hours lifting weights in the university training room. Apparently I was more involved with my exterior than my interior, as I kept complaining about the thorns.

One evening, over dinner, my roommate Danny looked me dead in the eye and said "Oechsli, you really have a terrible attitude!" I attempted to protest but he sharply cut me off saying, "You're always putting people down. Nothing is ever right because you seem to think you know it all. Well, I've got news for you—you don't even know that you are a real negative person who's hard to be around!" Then he got up and left the room.

There was no working partnership between us, we were just two friends trying to grow into adults. But what a wake-up call Danny gave me. My best friend was telling me that I was drag to be around! He was actually giving me feedback, although he didn't know how to give it constructively or offer constructive advice, Danny was holding me accountable for my attitude. I was grumbling about thorns, instead of being thankful for the roses.

Attitude Realization

That evening changed my life. Danny probably never realized what an impact he made on my inner being. Prior to his feedback, I thought my attitude was great. I knew that I was a wise guy and liked to poke fun, but I never realized that I was actually a negative person. The rest of that evening was spent in quiet reflection as I painfully admitted to myself that Danny was right. All my joking, put downs, wise cracks, and cynical remarks were an effort to build up my lack of self-esteem at the expense of others. What was most amazing was how blind I was to myself. Have you ever had a similar experience? Many people initially deny this realization.

As you prepare your life for high level achievement, it's time to make absolutely certain that neither you nor your partner have any attitudinal blind spots. There is no foolproof method for accomplishing this. Often just a good heart-to-heart, as my roommate had with me, is sufficient.

Because your success as a salesperson, spouse, parent, friend, neighbor depends primarily on your attitudes toward yourself, I want you to concentrate on reshaping any negative and self-defeating attitudes that you have into winning ones.

To help facilitate this process, and provide somewhat of a structured beginning for your working partnership discussion, I want you to complete the following Winning Attitude Profile.

This will help you create a more accurate picture of your current attitudes, identify areas in which your attitudes can be improved, and elicit the feedback, support, and *accountability* of your working partner.

WAP: Winning Attitude Profile

Instructions: This profile is designed to gauge your responses to situations relevant to winning the inner game of selling, personal and professional growth. The objective is to assist you to become aware of your own attitude and the effect it has on your income-producing abilities.

For best results, answer each question honestly as you are today, not as you would like to be. You will only be hurting your earning potential if you don't get full benefit from this profile. Use your working partner for feedback in guarding against blind spots.

After reading each statement, circle the number under the phrase which best describes your opinion.

	Strongly Agree	Mildly Agree	Mildly Disagree	Strongly Disagree
1. I often question my choice of career.	4	3	2	1
2. I've yet to focus on developing my IQ's.	4	3	2	1
3. I catch myself focusing on objections rather than my goals.	4	3	2	1
4. I have yet to really commit to pay the price to be the best.	4	3	2	1
5. I often doubt myself and my abilities.	4	3	2	1
6. I have trouble believing I can double my income.	4	3	2	1
7. I tend to take rejection personally.	4	3	2	1
8. I tend to dwell on my mistakes.	4	3	2	1
9. I have difficulty prospecting consistently.	4	3	2	1

10. I feel as though there is tremendous pressure to perform.	4	3	2	1
11. I wish I was more atten-tive to my family.	4	3	2	1
12. I'm reluctant to share my true inner dreams/ goals with my spouse.	4	3	2	1
13. I criticize my children more than compliment them.	4	3	2	1
14. I go out of my way to make others feel good about themselves.	1	2	3	4
15. I truly enjoy people.	1	2	3	4

Scoring the WAP: You will determine your WAP score by adding all the numbers you have circled.

Maximum Score = 60   My Score _____

Score

60 — 53   You better invest two hours a day to reshaping your attitude. Develop a daily checklist with your working partner. Your attitude is holding you back in a terrible way. Your potential is unlimited!

52 — 45   You will be able to double your income and your personal ac-complishments through attitude development. Make it a top priority with your partner.

44 — 36   Average; your attitude is holding you back in the same fash-ion of most salespeople. Recognize your strengths and weak-nesses. Discuss these at your weekly meetings.

35 — 21   Your attitude is a valuable asset! With a little bit of work you will be able to control your destiny. Help your working part-ner develop an equally strong attitude.

20 —   Please write to me! I can learn from you. Your duty is to trans-fer winning the inner game of selling to every salesperson you encounter. The sky is the limit!

After you've completed this profile with your partner, and you agree on the assessment of your attitude, make a commitment to change one weakness per week.

Areas For Improvement:

Review the individual items on the Profile and determine specific areas that you need to develop, strengthen, and enhance in your efforts to eliminate procrastination and improve performance. If you:

Circled **4**, you've identified an area to **develop.**

Circled **3**, you've identified an area to **strengthen.**

Circled **2**, you've identified an area to **enhance.**

Select *three areas* to work on between now and your next group meeting. List them below and discuss them with your partner.

#1— _____

#2— _____

#3— _____

Working Partner Discussion: Your attitude, not aptitude, will determine how far and long you travel on your success journey. Commit with your partner to keep a positive, good-natured, confident, hopeful, caring, courageous and sharing attitude. You both will radiate sunshine and fresh air wherever you go, with whomever you touch. You will enjoy good health and cheer in everything you do.

Conversely, make certain to avoid all people with negative attitudes as if they were lepers! Their despondent, fearful, anxious and resentful mental attitude, whether intended or not, will bring you down. This is the law of attraction and suggestion.

It has been well documented that General Grant, leading up to Appomattox, was suffering terribly from rheumatism. But as soon as it was announced to him that General Lee was prepared to surrender, his elation provided total and immediate freedom from his rheumatism for a good length of time. General Grant's attitude dominated his deteriorating physical condition.

Commit to reshaping your attitudes and you will attract people and events of a similar positive nature. At the same time, be observant of the salespeople in your company suffering from a problem with their attitude. Notice how often deals tend to fall through for them, how often they catch a head cold. Our attitude determines our luck. The law of attraction is as natural as night following day.

Always be cognizant of moods, yours and others. The human spirit, in the conscious state, is primarily a matter of mood.

All the inner workings of your psyche impact your emotional state. Through understanding and controlling many of these factors in yourself, you will be better able to recognize and discuss them with your partner, and ultimately communicate on a higher level with your prospects and customers. This is a valuable skill that you will master naturally as a result of recognizing and reshaping your attitudes.

Understand first, then be understood

Sam, a young medical supply salesman, told me this embarrassing story after I finished a public seminar. He sold primarily to hospitals, but often had to close the deal with a physician. It was a lucrative career as long as he could maintain the attitude to deal with stressed-out doctors.

Sam recounts this one situation: "I had been calling on this hospital for three years. I had a decent relationship, but it was always difficult to get hold of the appropriate doctor to make a decision. I knew I could be doing more business with them. I had this X-ray scanner, the latest high tech item that I knew would save them money. It took me two months to get hold of the radiologist who would make the buying decision. We had discussed this over the phone, I had sent him all the literature, and he said he was ready to do business."

Then Sam sighed and continued, "This is where it went downhill. I realized during my appointment with Dr. Paul that he was preoccupied. He was in a anxious mood. Because I too was anxious, I failed to recognize this and continued to push to my X-ray machine. I guess I wasn't paying attention to his feelings, because he asked me to leave and said if I said one more word, he would make certain I never sold a piece of equipment in the entire city."

This story had a happier ending. Sam never did sell the X-ray scanner to that physician. The hospital was in the process of being sold to a competitor—hence Dr. Paul's change in attitude. Sam realized his mistake, made amends with Dr. Paul. Because he worked on his attitude so he could better understand Dr. Paul's, he has started a side-line venture with Dr. Paul. Sam sells both the equipment and Dr. Paul's over-reading service to hospitals within a 300-mile radius.

Understand first, then be understood. Because Sam took the time to understand his anxieties in trying to sell this machine, he was able to understand Dr. Paul's anxieties about job security. The result was a business venture in which everybody prospered.

"Depression first maims the mind and then kills the body," says a proverb from India. Your challenge is to attract the events and the people who share your similar success attitude into your life. Dr. Paul might have been depressed about the sale of the hospital, but when exposed to the right attitude, he was able to find new life.

Below is a list of 24 personality characteristics that can be attributed to attitude. Go over this list with your partner. It is by no means all-inclusive, so let your attitude fuel your journey!

Winning Attitude Characteristics:

Amiable	Patience	Understanding	Fair
Benevolent	Temperance	Gentle	Peaceful
Honesty	Tolerance	Listening	Values
Humble	Courtesy	Punctuality	God
Enthusiastic	Love	Hygiene	Family
Kindness	Humor	Appearance	Decisive
Loyalty	Tactfulness	Charitable	Courage

Allow me to end this discussion on developing a winning attitude with a saying by Confucius: "Behave towards everyone as if receiving a great guest."

With that thought fresh in your mind, move on to take control over your programming cycle.

Wrap-Up

- Your attitude will determine your success journey.
- Attitude, not aptitude, generates success.
- Beware of attitudinal blind spots.
- Work through the Winning Attitude Profile with your working partner.
- Commit to reshaping one attitudinal weakness per week.
- Remember the laws of suggestion and attraction.
- "Know thy self."—Socrates

IMPORTANT STUFF!

1. List below the stuff you found important in this chapter.

   _____

   _____

2. What do you want to change? _____

   _____

   _____

3. When are you going to change it? _____

   _____

   _____

4. What are you going to enhance?_____

   _____

   _____

5. How are you going to enhance it? _____

   _____

   _____

Chapter 12

HOW TO CONTROL YOUR
PROGRAMMING CYCLE—YOUR ATTITUDE

How did you score on the Winning Attitude Profile? Was there much similarity between your answers and your partner's answers? Most working partners are so similar in scores that it's a bit eerie. But after all, we're all much more similar than dissimilar.

If either of you scored well on the Winning Attitude Profile, you're probably already benefiting from a positive programming cycle. Attitude always mirrors programming. Your programming cycle is the cause, your attitude is the effect. Although they appear to overlap, and everyone knows someone with a bad attitude, the programming cycle is the cause. Everything you have accomplished in life, all that you do, is a direct result of the thoughts that have been programmed into your subconscious mind.

The following exercise will give you a feeling for how simple and direct this cause and effect relationship really is. You need to pay close attention to your thoughts. A little computer jargon helps paint a good picture of the programming cycles in your mind.

The Garbage In/Garbage Out Model
(Negative Programming Cycle vs. Positive Programming Cycle)

The oft-used phrase from computer technology, "garbage in/garbage out," provides a good working example of how the conscious and the subconscious interrelate. You can get a good feel for how the negative and positive programming cycles evolve through the following examples. Complete the model with other examples based on your own experience:

Garbage In (Misinformation)	Garbage Out (Behavior)
1. "I don't like prospecting."	1. Call reluctance.
2. "I'll never achieve my goals."	2. Lack of achievement drive.
3. (Write your own.)	3. (Write your own.)

No one deceives us more than our own thoughts.

—Silesian proverb

Goal-Oriented Thoughts

Positive Input	Positive Output (Behavior)
1. "I love to prospect!"	1. Consistent prospecting activity.
2. "I always achieve my goals!"	2. High achievement drive, doing whatever is needed.
3. (Write your own.)	3. (Write your own.)

As I'm sure you're already aware, and the garbage-in/garbage-out exercise simply reminded you, repeated negative thoughts can kill your sales career. It has been my observation that far too many salespeople are victims of the negative programming cycle. And, they are totally unaware of the fact. Cynical salespeople waste a lot of time convincing themselves that they're just "telling it like it is."

Now *I'm* going to tell you like it is. The number one bad habit that keeps salespeople from realizing their earning potential is the negative programming cycle. Garbage in/garbage out!

Working Partner Exercise:

List the most common garbage-in statements that you hear on a daily basis. They can be from the office, from home or from your country club. Compare lists and evaluate the success of the people making these statements. Are they people you admire or are they unhappy losers?

Make a commitment to avoid these people and garbage-in statements. You can't control what other people talk about, but you can control who you listen to and talk with.

Public Bad Habit #1

Since very few people have been taught how to use their conscious thoughts, most people abuse them by thinking too much. Think of the last time you thought, "I hate the phone!" There's probably a good chance you never made the call. And if you did, you weren't as confident as you needed to be. Why?

Too much thinking leads to negative thinking. As you overplayed your thoughts about calling this prospect, doubt started to creep in; you knew all the reasons they wouldn't want to do business with you. You replayed all the possible objections. Then you started worrying. Not only did you worry about this prospect rejecting you, you worried about how your selling career was progressing, you worried about being able to provide for your family, you worried. . . .

Whether you worried along the lines of my scenario, or you had one of your own, negative thoughts lead to worry. Anytime you find yourself worrying about something, you are actually killing any type of productive behavior. Worry is a cancer to productivity!

Negative programming

This is true in every aspect of life. I recall a businessman, a successful entrepreneur, who came to me for help in overcoming his fear of speaking in public. He was absolutely "petrified" of the mere thought, and it cost him a huge sum of money.

This is what happened: Mr. Simmons agreed, against his better judgment, to give a talk to a local charitable organization. He agreed because an executive for a large corporation, who he had been trying to do business with, asked if he would share his expertise on team building. Feeling he would jeopardize his chance of getting the business, Simmons agreed to give the speech.

The date was six weeks off and Simmons had it on his mind constantly. The closer the date, the more the anxiety; he'd break out in a cold sweat, had trouble sleeping, and couldn't concentrate on his business.

Poor Simmons made the cardinal sin of any speaker—he failed to show up! The meeting was without a speaker, the corporate executive was furious, and Simmons was afraid to show his face. Why?

His conscious thoughts had programmed his subconscious mind so negatively that he could not give that speech, no matter how hard he tried. Yes, he should have called, but up until the last minute he was still consciously planning to give the speech—but he couldn't.

Has anything of this nature ever happened to you? Did you ever promise a prospect you would get back to them and didn't? Have you ever received a hot referral from a client or customer who had already notified the prospect that you would call, and you never called?

Working Partner Exercise:

The following is an exercise to be performed with your working partner.

Negative Programming Interference: Your example

Event sabotaged by programming cycle: _____

_____

_____

Actual negative programming (repeated thoughts): _____

_____

_____

Resulting action/inaction: _____

_____

_____

Future prevention tactics: _____

_____

_____

Working partnership:

Accountability _____

Feedback _____

Support _____

By recognizing and taking control of your programming cycle, you will automatically perform as you would really like to perform. This way you can work smart. Too many people wear themselves out working hard, but like Mr. Simmons, they were programmed wrong from the start. Not until they change their programming cycle will they be able to work smart.

How negative programming starts

It's interesting how negative programming can develop. Mr. Simmons can vividly remember being humiliated by his seventh grade English teacher for giggling when attempting to recite a poem to the class. That scene scared him for 27 years. That was classic negative programming.

What programming is holding you back? Were you told that you would never amount to anything if you didn't go to college, a particular college, medical school? Were you told selling isn't an honorable profession? Were you told that very few people make it in your business? I want you to think about your current Winning Attitude Profile, and think of it as your Programming Cycle Profile, as I outline the #1 bad habit:

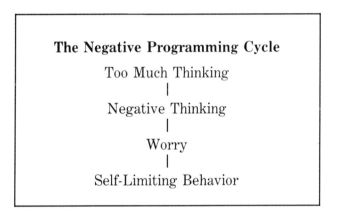

Your programming cycle is a product of your life up to this point. It's learned behavior, a habit that you probably have been unaware of most of the time. Before you panic about your programming cycle, I've got some good news for you. All habits can be changed in only 21 days. You can change a lifetime programming habit within 21 days, if you are aggressively committed to changing. This is where your weekly partnership meetings will give you a significant advantage. Because, let's face it, changing habits is not easy.

From this moment on, realize that your future, your success in selling, will be influenced directly on your decision to control your programming cycle. I will teach you, coach you, show you the way, but you have to make the decision. "I am in control of my future!" needs to be the theme, not "I'll see what happens."

Think of your hero. Did your hero stand aside and let the events of the world dictate his or her level of accomplishment? Of course not! Personal responsibility was accepted for his or her thoughts, focus and programming of subconscious mind. Now it's your turn.

Think about your current Winning Attitude Profile as I outline the #1 success habit.

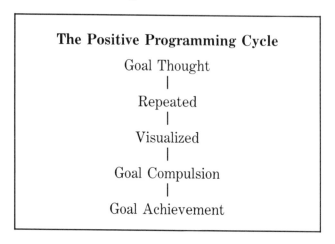

Let me repeat; you can't control the thoughts that enter your mind. But it's your success responsibility to control the thoughts you dwell on. These repeated thoughts determine whether you function in a positive or negative programming cycle. It's that simple. Simple, yes, easy? No change is easy.

The consequences of the programming cycle you choose can be devastating! Two members of a financial planning firm I did a consulting project with provide an excellent illustration. Jack and Greg had been in the financial services field for 12 and 15 years respectively. They were in their mid- to late-thirties. Jack was more of an aggressive salesman, and Greg was more of an expert in the technical aspects of finances.

Jack wanted to prospect a major business in the area and, knowing he didn't have the technical expertise to handle in-depth questions, he asked Greg to come with him. They were going to work jointly with this prospect and split the commissions—which would be very sizable.

After the initial interview with this business, the difference in their programming cycles was obvious.

Positive cycle: Jack's mind was racing over all the possibilities, calculating all the varying commissions that could be earned.

Negative cycle: Greg was annoyed with how impersonal and brief their meeting was. After two follow-up appointments were cancelled, he gave up. "I want nothing to do with these arrogant people! I told you they would never do business with us!"

They re-scheduled three more times with Jack, but he hung in there, as if he'd been in the audience during Winston Churchill's "Never,

never, never, give up" speech. Jack kept focusing on the potential earnings and persisted.

By focusing on his goal thoughts, Jack could handle all the little setbacks along the way. His goal was much stronger than the irritation of a cancelled meeting.

Greg, on the other hand, could not handle the adversity. His focus was on the setbacks, and when they occurred they validated his negative attitude.

Rewards of the positive programming cycle

Fifteen months later, Jack collected the largest commission check of his career. Through his goal-focused patience, persistence and bonding with his prospect, he sold the entire gamut of financial services. Greg never participated.

Control your programming cycle and you control your destiny.

Developing your positive programming cycle

The first step is to reflect on your life and your career in sales, and determine what changes would make you more productive. Use your hero and the IQ/SQ gauge to help stimulate your thoughts. What changes would help you become the success in selling that you want to be? From these, you will write your own self-affirmation statements. Work through your statements with your partner for feedback.

The precise wording is critical, as it will determine what you program in your subconscious mind. Your subconscious is extremely literal; remember, it takes every message at face value. If you tell yourself, "I am no longer lazy," your subconscious interprets it as though you are lazy. So you need to talk to yourself about what you want, as if it were real now. So you say instead, "I work hard every day."

Properly worded affirmations will enable you to lie to yourself and enjoy the benefits. The most immediate benefit is the boost in self-esteem. The following is a guide to insuring that your affirmations have maximum impact:

1. *Personal.* Begin each statement with "I am," "I have," "It's easy for me." This will direct your statements internally, as you can affirm change in yourself, but you cannot affirm change in another person.

    Example: Wrong—"My boss will praise me for my high closing ratio."

           Right— "I am a closing machine, achieving my goals!"

2. *Positive.* Leave your problems behind! Always word your affirmations by emphasizing what you desire.

Example: Wrong—"I'm no longer call reluctant."
Right— "I make 20 prospecting calls every day."

3. *Present Tense.* All your affirmations must be worded as if they are true now, even though you have yet to accomplish them.

Example: Wrong—"I will become successful."
Right— "I am successful!"

4. *Comparison Free.* You must "tend thy own garden," as Voltaire told us in his masterpiece, *Candide.* You can develop a false sense of reality by evaluating yourself in relation to others. Admire and emulate the IQ's and SQ's of your hero or mentor, this is a role model. But do not compare!

Example: Wrong—"I'm going to sell more than Mary."
Right— "I earned $10,000 in commissions this month."

Another good rule to keep in mind when your write your affirmations is to use words of action and emotion whenever appropriate. This will help accelerate the changes. Use words like: quick, powerful, terrific, enjoy, love, strong. . . .

Write your own self-affirmations

Think of seven specific change areas, because you are going to use seven statements to develop your positive programming cycle. This is a very powerful exercise, and I must again emphasize balance in your goals. You need to include statements about your personal, family, and spiritual areas, as well as your professional affirmations. Spend time alone working on the balance of your life, and then spend time discussing this with your partner.

If you don't balance your statements, you can easily focus entirely on being a money-making machine. But you will be terribly unhappy. You will jeopardize your family, your health, and even your integrity.

Think of an area of change, and imagine yourself enjoying the change as if it has already occurred. Then write out what you imagined, in your own words, and you have your own personalized affirmation.

Examples:
Change Area: I want to make 20 prospecting calls every day.
Image: See yourself making 20 calls.
Affirmation: I make 20 prospecting calls every day.

Change Area: I want to lose weight.
Image: See yourself healthy and fit at your natural weight.
Affirmation: I am healthy and fit and enjoy my natural weight!

Write your own.

Change Area: _____

_____

Image: _____

_____

Affirmation: _____

_____

Change Area: _____

_____

Image: _____

_____

Affirmation: _____

_____

The following are samples of affirmations that might help get you started. Let me clarify one point about balance and change. One of my affirmations is "I am a loving, caring husband and father." This does not mean that I'm currently a lousy father; I'm a good father. This affirmation serves as a balance to some other career-focused statements that could possibly get me to put my family lower on my subconscious priority list. Because of the power of affirmations, family, spiritual, and health should always be mentioned.

Sample affirmations

Sales Success:
- I am a prospecting machine!
- I always provide quality, value and service!
- I am the best!
- I am committed to my daily mind power, goal-setting exercise.
- I am a closing machine!
- I always ask for and get referrals from every customer.

Family:
- I am a loving caring spouse and parent!
- I always make time for my family!
- I spend quality time with my children every day!
- I always take time to read with my children!
- I involve my family in all areas of my life!
- I spend quiet conversation time with my spouse!

Health:
- I am healthy and fit mentally, physically, and spiritually.
- I exercise every day.
- I am in total control of food and drink.
- I sleep soundly every night and wake rested and refreshed.
- I treat my body as it were my temple.
- I am relaxed, confident, and full of positive energy.

Spiritual:
- I am committed to God and my church!
- I live by the golden rule!
- I always instill spiritual beliefs in my children.
- I do what is right!
- I spend time in prayer and reading the Bible daily.
- I am committed to being the best person God made me to be!

Please understand the sample affirmations above are only samples. My intention is to stimulate your thoughts while showing you the proper wording and structure. By no means do these samples reflect any particular religion, culture or business. This is for your personal customization.

You're now ready to learn how to use your own personal affirmations to make your own self-programming cassette tape. This will become one of your most powerful self-help tools, accelerating the creation of the most important success habit known to mankind: The Positive Programming Cycle!

Wrap-Up

- Most salespeople are victims of the negative programming cycle.
- Everybody has negative thoughts, but not everybody is in the negative programming cycle.

- The negative programming cycle is the #1 Bad Habit. It holds more people back than all others combined!
- Too much thinking, negative thinking, worry is self-limiting behavior.
- Your most powerful success habit is The Positive Programming Cycle!
- Goal thought—repeated—visualized—goal compulsion—goal achievement.
- Determine the changes you need to make you a more productive salesperson.
- Design affirmation statements to facilitate the programming of this change into your subconscious.
- Specific wording of your affirmations is critical: personal, present tense, positive and comparison free.

IMPORTANT STUFF!

1.   List below the stuff you found important in this chapter.

_____

_____

2.   What do you want to change? _____

_____

_____

3.   When are you going to change it? _____

_____

_____

4.   What are you going to enhance?_____

_____

_____

5.   How are you going to enhance it? _____

_____

_____

Chapter 13

MAKING YOUR MOST POWERFUL SELF-HELP TAPE

You're now equipped to control your internal tapes. Those recordings that have been playing in your head for so long are now going to be re-recorded by you! This is exciting! I get goose bumps just writing about it! You now have the power to change your life. Sounds great, doesn't it?!

But simply reading through these exercises, intellectually understanding them, and discussing them with your working partner is not enough. If this was the extent of your involvement, you would soon be overwhelmed by your old tapes and forfeit the control over your destiny. I've seen the best intentions go down the drain because of failure to act on the contents of this chapter. So please, put an hour aside with your partner, and make your tapes!

I've been referring to the programming in your subconscious as an internal script, a tape that is continually playing in your mind that determines your behavior. As you've learned in the previous chapter, most people are held back because of one big bad habit—the negative programming cycle. As you worked through the affirmation exercises, and discussed them with your working partner, I'm sure you were able to understand how the wording of your self-talk impacts your subconscious programming.

I am confident that both of you were able to identify change areas and strategically word corresponding self-affirmation statements to give maximum impact on your internal re-programming.

155

Therefore, you are now intellectually prepared to change your internal scripts, your programming cycle, your tapes. Is this change possible? Yes! But it is not easy. Very few people will master the inner game of selling on intellect alone, even with the help of a partner. Changing the scripts in your mind requires systematic aggressive action on an emotional level. This is why it's so important for you to make your own self-programming cassette.

Your Personal Programming Tape

Your affirmations, your voice, your mind, your success! Nothing is more powerful than listening to yourself recite strategically spaced and repeated personal statements, statements concerning exactly what you want out of life.

When most people listen to their voice on a recording for the first time, whether it's leaving a message on an answering machine, dictating a letter, or whatever, they immediately dislike how it sounds. This has always amused me because the most powerful medium to our subconscious minds is the sound of our own voice.

Think back to the last time you got excited about the possibilities of closing a big sale. You couldn't really verbalize out loud because you were still with your prospect, but there was going to be a big fat commission, and you were excitedly talking to yourself about it. Could you hear exactly what you were thinking? You bet you could! You probably didn't give it any thought, but your subconscious mind heard your thoughts as clearly as if you had spoken out loud.

Whether it's cursing under your breath, reflectively thinking to yourself, or silent prayer, your subconscious hears your tone of voice, inflection, mood and sincerity. I am going to give you two statements of opposite emotion. Say them to yourself as if you were thinking of them naturally:

1. "What a beautiful day!"

2. "I wish that creep would stop tailgating me!"

What did your mind do? Not only did you hear yourself as if you had said those statements aloud, you probably got an emotional feeling of being there. Now repeat the two statements out loud, as if you were really stepping outside to a wonderful day, and driving on the highway with some jerk following you much too closely.

Did you feel more powerful in your conviction when you spoke out loud? Could you feel closer to really being there? Most people can because of the addition of the auditory element from your self-talk.

Your voice is your most powerful medium

Nothing has more impact on your behavior than you. This is why there is so much hype in motivational speakers, manipulative sales trainers and television evangelists. They are merely external forces at work trying to juice you up for some short-term behavior. Naturally, this never works, because you will ultimately behave in direct accordance to your internal scripts, your programming.

Since your voice has the most impact on you, let's put it on a tape recording. Yes, a common tape recorder can replace all the hype I have mentioned. By recording your personalized self-affirmation statements with your enthusiasm and emotion, all you have to do is drive down the highway of life and listen. Your voice, your message, your mind, your future . . . your success journey!

Let's make a tape.

You can use the affirmation statements you developed in the previous chapter or you can create new ones, but you will need seven self-affirmation statements. Because you are reading this book to assist you in your professional growth, and we have agreed that this must go arm in arm with personal growth, I am going to recommend that you have four statements pertaining to your professional sales career. Use the remaining three to round out the balance in your life: personal, family and spiritual.

I'm repeating myself because of the power involved with the tool you're about to create. I know it's hard for you to imagine anything that powerful, but this will be *that powerful!* It would be unethical for me to share this exercise with you without insisting upon balance. You're about to get involved with a tool that must be used properly. It's extremely important to have balance in your life.

Discuss this with your partner. Make certain you both appreciate the need for balance. This tape will have such a powerful impact, that if you fail to incorporate balance into the recording, you could easily ruin your life. In my seminars and workshops, I never allow anyone to make this tape without including balance.

I call this self-programming cassette your "7-7-7 Tape." Essentially, it is seven self-affirmation statements repeated seven times, with each repetition spaced seven seconds apart. Your entire tape will consist of 49 statements; seven different statements repeated seven times each.

Now what is the purpose of this spaced repetition? Why seven statements? Why seven seconds apart? Since your mind thinks in images and you converse in words, the seven-second pause between repetitions allows your mind to naturally create the images of the affirmation you've just recited. Then by repeating that same affirmation seven seconds later with another seven-second pause, your corresponding images not only become much stronger, they begin to have a re-programing effect on your subconscious.

Repetition has often been said to be the mother of learning. With that in mind, consider spaced repetition as the fathering of re-scripting the tapes in your mind. If you start repeating more than seven statements, there is a chance you will be confusing yourself and losing the emotional impact of this powerful exercise.

Once, during an in-house program, a salesperson returned to our second session with 18 self-affirmation statements. The group had spent an entire week working on their seven statements for this recording session. This particular salesman claimed he needed so much re-scripting that he couldn't work with any less than 18. I then asked him to share with the group, from memory, all of his 18 statements. He could only recite seven.

The reason I have selected seven repetitions with seven-second spacing is for simplicity. Quite frankly, it is easier for people to remember. You could repeat each statement nine times and pause for ten seconds between. But seven repetitions and seven-second pauses provide the impact power on the subconscious that is necessary for re-scripting. This will provide you with approximately a 15-minute recording. If you cut back on the number of repetitions or shortened the pauses, you would lessen the impact on your subconscious mind. Your objective is to maximize the impact!

Does this really work?

Many salespeople initially categorize this 7-7-7 Tape with the subliminal tapes that are sold everywhere today. This is a big mistake. First of all, the concept behind a subliminal message is that it is not audible on a conscious level, rather a preconscious level. Although there is validity to that concept, two concerns immediately surface:

1. The validity of the program you purchase. For those who must purchase a subliminal product, I recommend Denis Waitley's "The Subliminal Winner," produced by Nightingale Conant. Denis Waitley and Nightingale Conant are both extremely credible.

2. The most powerful programming tool for your mind is your message, your self-talk, and your voice. I've met thousands of salespeople who wasted money on subliminal products because they expected the tapes to automatically make a change in their life. This never happens!

Jack had tried subliminal tapes, and so had a number of his salespeople. A sales manager for a large insurance company, Jack had developed a case of call reluctance. His personal production was down, recruiting was off, and he thought he'd infected his staff with his problem with prospecting.

His entire office attended a public seminar I was conducting for a local merchant's association. Jack called me a couple of weeks later. "I wasn't sure about making my tape, but my people were all hyped up so I made mine out of obligation. I listened to it driving to and from the office. Three days later, I made a major appointment with a powerful person that I had bumped into on the golf course one day. My initial inclination was '*No*, he's not going to want to be bothered with you.' But I started hearing my voice on my 7-7-7 Tape saying, 'I'm a prospecting machine,' and I just went over to him, introduced myself, and got an appointment for next week."

What excited Jack most was experiencing the subtle difference between doing and walking away. He almost chickened out with this prospect, but instead he got a new referral. Equally as important, Jack is re-building his self-esteem and confidence by *doing*. As he listens to his messages he's re-programming the tapes in his head. He had no such experience with subliminals.

One last thought on subliminal tapes. They can be very soothing and serve as good background music/sound to your goal programming exercise in the next chapter. If you use them to complement your efforts, I can accept them. As for total effort, I've never seen much benefit.

Four steps—step by step

I have listed seven affirmation statements as I want you to write yours on a 3 × 5″ index card. Use mine only as examples; if some of the statements reflect your needs, feel free to use them. But please put thought into your other statements. No two people will have identical winning inner selling needs. Your tape should reflect your personal and professional needs. This is what will make it most powerful and effective.

STEP ONE: Write out seven self-affirmation statements.

1. I am a prospecting machine!

2. I always get referrals from my clients/customers!

3. I am committed to my daily synergistic goal setting exercise!

4. I always provide superior quality, value and service to my clients and customers!

5. I am healthy and fit mentally, physically and spiritually!

6. I am a loving caring husband and father!

7. I am full of confidence and always live by the golden rule!

STEP TWO: Test your voice for clarity, volume and cadence.

Record your first statement three times, just as if you were making the entire tape: I am a prospecting machine! (1-2-3-4-5-6-7) I am a prospecting machine! (1-2-3-4-5-6-7) I am a prospecting machine! (1-2-3-4-5-6-7)

STEP THREE: Replay your recorded affirmations and make the proper adjustments.

1. Speak slowly in a clear, audible manner.

2. Speak slightly louder than normal conversation.

3. Change your voice inflection to enhance the images created.

4. Use the second hand of a clock, a digital watch or simply count to seven for timing your pauses.

STEP FOUR: Record your 7-7-7 Self-Programming Tape. Note: The following example will use the seven affirmation statements above.

1. I am a prospecting machine! (1-2-3-4-5-6-7) I am a prospecting machine! (1-2-3-4-5-6-7) I am a prospecting machine! (1-2-3-4-5-6-7) I am a prospecting machine! (1-2-3-4-5-6-7) I am a prospecting machine! (1-2-3-4-5-6-7) I am a prospecting machine! (1-2-3-4-5-6-7) I am a prospecting machine! (1-2-3-4-5-6-7)

2. I always get referrals from my clients! (1-2-3-4-5-6-7) I always get referrals from my clients! (1-2-3-4-5-6-7) I always get referrals from my clients! (1-2-3-4-5-6-7) I always get referrals from my clients! (1-2-3-4-5-6-7) I always get referrals from my clients! (1-2-3-4-5-6-7) I always get referrals from my clients! (1-2-3-4-5-6-7) I always get referrals from my clients! (1-2-3-4-5-6-7)

3. Continue this process for all seven statements.

Let this 7-7-7 Self-Programming Tape serve as a passive tool while you're driving or involved in other activities. You don't have to listen to every word. This is the magic of this re-scripting tool; your conscious mind can be drifting off to others thoughts as you listen, but your subconscious will always be creating those powerful images.

You never have to force your images. The spacing is designed for the images to occur naturally, and they will. At times, you will find yourself naturally paying closer attention; on other occasions, your mind will wander. Let it, this is only normal. As long as you listen to the tape on a daily basis, you will re-script your mind on an emotional level. You will be taking a major shortcut in changing the tapes that govern your life.

Re-program every 21 days

Since it takes 21 days of aggressive activity to change a habit, I have found it most effective to change the tape every 21 days. I know, this requires time and energy. But that is exactly what is going to contribute to ultimate success!

I've discovered over the years of teaching salespeople the art of making their personal 7-7-7 Tapes that the initial excitement sometimes turns into boredom. Some people get tired of hearing the same message, especially if they have grown beyond some of their original affirmations.

For best results, re-record your tape every 21 days. This does not mean every affirmation must be changed. I always keep two the same: "I am healthy and fit mentally, physically and spiritually!" and "I am a loving, caring husband and father!" You will probably have some that remain constant, but re-record the entire tape anyway. You will always control your internal tapes; therefore, continue to challenge yourself with growth.

Third-Person Programming

For those of you who really enjoy the idea of being at the controls of your own programming, third-person affirmation statements are a tremendous boost. After you finish recording your forty-ninth statement, you can fill the remainder of the cassette side with compliments about yourself. For example:

You're the best! (1-2-3-4-5-6-7) You're the best! (1-2-3-4-5-6-7)

You are an excellent role model!

You always do what is right!

161

And so on . . . each third-person affirmation should be repeated at least twice. None of us receive enough compliments, so why not compliment ourselves? Many salespeople enjoy the third-person affirmation so much they make an entire tape of third-person compliments.

Remember, the better you feel about yourself the more successful you will be. Proactive people aren't going to wait for their bosses, neighbors, or spouses to make them feel good; they are going to do that themselves. Hence the value of third-person affirmations. They are really compliments to yourself that you would love to receive. So go now and receive them!

Working partner and spouse affirmations

Building on your third-party affirmations, you can create real power by having your working partner recite your affirmations along with you on the second side of your cassette. This duet will go something like this: You: "I'm the best!" (1-2-3-4-5-6-7) Working Partner: "Matt, you're the best!" (1-2-3-4-5-6-7) You: "I'm the best!" (1-2-3-4-5-6-7) Working Partner: "Matt, you're the best!" And so on for all of your statements. It becomes real magic when you can enlist your spouse to help with your recording. This feedback was given to me by Dan Erler with Management Recruiters International. About a month after I conducted a seminar for his company, Dan called me to give a progress report.

Already one of the top producers in the company, it was interesting to listen to him talk about how much his production was up. He was more than doubling his activity, but that wasn't what had him most excited. He'd gotten creative and wanted my opinion, "Matt, I was thinking about including my wife on another tape, simply repeating my statements after me. She listened to my tape and was impressed." He paused, and then asked, "What do you think?"

My response was immediate and affirmative! I loved it! My personal "7-7-7 Tape" has since turned into a stronger dose of magic, as I asked my wife Sandy to help me with my recording. It is amazing how we learn. This is one of the most powerful tools for not only winning the inner game of selling, but for strengthening a marriage. Think of the enhanced communication, empathy and love that can be generated! Wow! Heck, this concept can improve any relationship.

Wrap-up

- Your voice is most powerful to you.
- You need to be aggressive to change your programming cycle.
- Balance is essential to your "7-7-7 Tape."
- Change your tape every 21 days.
- Listen to your tape daily.
- Actively accept control of your mind.
- Use third-person affirmations.
- Record your working partner using third-person affirmations.
- Record your spouse using third-person affirmations.

IMPORTANT STUFF!

1. List below the stuff you found important in this chapter.

    _____

    _____

2. What do you want to change? _____

    _____

    _____

3. When are you going to change it? _____

    _____

    _____

4. What are you going to enhance?_____

    _____

    _____

5. How are you going to enhance it? _____

    _____

    _____

Chapter 14

SELF-ESTEEM BOOSTERS

Let me start this chapter by asking you a question. In light of everything you've learned—working partners, role model, IQ/SQ's, recognizing your past, mapping your future, suggestive relaxation, synergistic goal setting, controlling your programming cycle—why is it that only a few people in sales become the real winners?

Masses of salespeople will still barely get by. What is necessary to commit faithfully to what you've already learned in the previous chapters?

High-Level Self-Esteem

We discovered that the qualities and characteristics of successful salespeople were IQ's, inner qualities. These people make the right things happen on the outside because they are making the right things happen inside themselves.

But here we're interested in why and how they make the right things happen inside themselves. How are they able to develop all of those IQ's? Why are they able to commit to goals, get themselves going each morning and work excitedly all day every day? How can they face all the setbacks, pressures and anxieties every salesperson faces, and still perform at consistently high levels? Why is it that some salespeople naturally score high on the Winning Attitude Profile?

What is so obvious and fascinating, because they are so often overlooked, are the qualities and characteristics that are vital to a successful salesperson and are found in virtually every successful person, regardless of their profession. Do people inherit success genes? Of course not!

Are some people just born to be salespeople? Zig Ziglar says "I've seen a lot of little boy babies, and I've seen a lot of little girl babies, but I've never yet seen anybody who was born a salesperson baby!"

Or, could it be possible that these high dollar salespeople are just lucky enough to always be at the right place at the right time with the right product? I know this thought has passed through your mind on occasion, but don't you believe it! If you've been selling very long, you know that luck has little or nothing to do with success. Like success in other professions, successful selling is something you do; not something that happens to you!

So what is that magic ingredient that separates the real winners at the selling game from the masses of salespeople who just barely get by—and who hate every minute of every day?

The Gold Coin of Self-Esteem

I like to refer to it as The Gold Coin of Self-Esteem. Harvard Medical School conducted a major study which determined that successful salespeople have certain basic psychological characteristics. The researchers wanted to know what traits it took to become successful at selling.

They discovered that the one trait which shows up most often in top salespeople is a strong, positive self-image. In other words, they found that the most vital ingredient for success in selling is that "you've gotta' like yourself."

That brings up such an obvious concept that I frequently refer to it as one of my radical ideas about winning the inner game of selling: "People who feel good about themselves produce good results!" The idea is not new with me. Napoleon communicated this clearly as he led his troops from victory to victory; Ken Blanchard talks about this in his outstanding book called *"The One Minute Manager."* Let me repeat it: "People who feel good about themselves produce good results!"

Sounds like a fairly common sense statement, doesn't it? It really doesn't seem very radical. Intellectually, most people would agree that people who feel good about themselves produce good results. But as Ben Franklin said in reference to "common sense" over two hundred years ago, "If it's so common, why is it that so few people possess it?" Well said, Benjamin!

What makes this so radical is that, true to Franklin's prose, common sense is precisely opposite of the way most sales managers, salespeople and parents act in their daily lives. Everybody knows that people who feel good about themselves produce good results. Yet reflect back on the last three meetings your sales manager conducted.

Did you feel good when it was over? Probably not. Reflect back to your childhood. How often do you recall your parents telling you how special you were, building you up, as opposed to reminding about everything you did wrong? It's plain to see how this common sense gets lost at an early stage. The long-term ramifications can be devastating.

What about our children?

In his book *The Path Of Least Resistance*, Robert Fritz cites a study done by a couple of behavioral psychologists. They wanted to determine what type of communication children ages four to seven were receiving from their primary adult figures; parents and teachers.

The psychologists outfitted a group of children in this age bracket with portable cassette players to record the communication these youngsters received from their role model figures. The results were an embarrassment, as well as very revealing. The children were hearing close to nine negative messages for every one sincere positive message! This is sad. How is your communication with the children in your life?

It is no wonder we're having so much trouble in our families and schools today. We're training our children to develop the #1 Bad Habit—the negative programming cycle. Of course, they're going to focus on their shortcomings if that is where they're directed by parents and teachers. Do you think many people will grow into adulthood with a strong self-image and healthy self-esteem with this scenario?

To motivate or demotivate

Let me share with you a recent experience that brings this message full circle. I was about to conduct a training program for a large office equipment company. Before my program began, I was discussing the agenda with the president of the company. He appeared excited about the program, and was telling me how pumped up all his managers and salespeople were. He went on to say how everyone really needed this message, the timing was perfect. Then, like somebody flipped a switch in his brain, he began bad-mouthing his employees.

"They're lazy, can't be trusted anymore, sometimes I think I should get rid of all of them and start over." Wow, he just expressed his true feelings, and his real leadership style—intimidation. It was obvious this company's president wasn't very pleased with the work habits of his employees, much like a parent looking at a report card full of C's.

Do you create an environment that motivates and builds self-esteem or does the opposite occur?

As the president introduced me, he did not sound like an enthusiastic leader ready to inspire his troops to greatness. Instead, he was condescending. He told his employees' his feelings about their laziness and poor performance. He blamed them for the expense of my program. Ouch!!

Everything turned out well in the end, but there were a few delicate moments. Interestingly, through discussing our role model relationship with our children, this president finally realized what he was doing to his company. Using a little "common sense" and a lot of courage, he closed my program with an apology for his leadership style, a commitment to change, and announced he was retaining my services to help him personally. It's never too late to change.

Unfortunately, there are millions of salespeople subjected to such demotivating behavior, without apology, every day. Self-esteem is bashed regularly, by prospects, customers and management.

So, if high level self-esteem is going to be, it's up to me! Right? Think about it. Except for your working partner, you cannot depend on others to build you up. How often has management put you down?

The typical sales manager and salesperson acts as if producing good results is what makes them feel good about themselves or deserving of kind words. In other words, when they make a big sale they feel great, they are praised! When they are rejected on a prospecting call, fail to close at the end of a presentation, or fail to meet their quota, they feel badly about themselves. They are reminded about it constantly.

Imagine a mother yelling at her baby as it falls trying to learn how to walk. Every time that little bundle of life takes a nose dive into the carpet, mother exclaims, "You're good for nothing, you're never going to learn how to walk!" I know that's farfetched; no one would ever think to act like that to a child learning how to walk. We applaud learning in youngsters; it's only after they're in school that most people forget how to communicate with children.

Praise becomes forgotten in the eternal quest for perfection, and students tend to be reminded every time they make a mistake.

Does this sound familiar? Does your boss treat you the way the president of the business equipment company treated his people? Are you treated with respect? Do you treat your children with respect, or do you focus on what they did wrong as opposed to what they did right? Everything you learn about winning the inner game of selling can be applied to your children—you're their "boss."

Here is another case of the obvious being overlooked. This is so fundamental, yet when can you remember a teacher emphasizing confidence? Can you recall a boss who always made people feel better about themselves? They are few and far between. That's why this message is so critical to your success. You must accept full responsibility for making yourself feel good. You must accept full responsibility for being confident. You are responsible for your achievement drive, because real motivation comes from within.

Working Partner Exercise:

The object of this exercise is to discuss your relationships and how they have an impact on your self-esteem, achievement drive and quality of life. Write a couple of sentences following each heading to discuss how you feel toward this person, how you act, and what you can control. Think of the control flame.

Mother: _____

_____

Father: _____

_____

Boss: _____

_____

Spouse: _____

_____

Children: _____

_____

Customers: _____

_____

Prospects: _____

_____

Friends: _____

_____

How good do you feel about *you?*

How do you feel about yourself? How can you tell if you feel good about yourself? You will find it very helpful to always be aware of the type of relationship you have with others. It's not your fault if someone else is not happy with life. But it is your fault if it is you and your life!

What is important is how we think and feel about ourselves; this we can control by what we do. This determines how good we are at whatever we are doing, whether it's in selling, or sports, or even personal relationships.

As Shakespeare said, "We know what we are, but not what we may be." Do you concentrate on your limitations, your failures, the negative energy of others? Or, are you beginning to think of what you might be? This simple point of focus can determine your fate, professionally and personally.

In the questions that follow you'll probably relate to some of the typical responses. That's okay, as long as you now consider yourself the co-creator of your life.

Because of the baggage many people carry, defenses are built in an attempt to cover up all shortcomings, and it becomes difficult to know how you really feel.

Building self-esteem, like any meaningful change, requires work, and that work must be outside of your existing comfort zone.

Here are some questions which can help you determine just how good you feel about yourself.

First, what do you say when someone asks you what you do for a living? Most salespeople will come out with something like "I'm in real estate," or "I'm a sales consultant," or they say, "I work for XYZ company!" Are you reluctant to come right out and tell someone, "I'm a salesperson"?

The reason most salespeople will tell you anything but that they are salespeople is that they are ashamed of what they do. But the real winners at the inner game of selling will look you square in the eye and tell you proudly, "I'm a salesperson!"

170

So the first clue to how good you feel about yourself is how proud you are about what you do every day. Later, I'm going to give you specific action steps that will allow you change the way you feel about what you do. For now, though, let's look at the second question that shows how you feel about yourself.

How hard is it to get yourself going and keep going all day? A study done by Columbia University found that the average salesperson spends less than 1½ hours each day actually selling. It also showed that the first sales call is usually made after 11 a.m. This doesn't mean that the average salesperson is lazy like the business equipment executive claimed, it's just that they hate making prospecting and sales calls.

Does this sometimes happen to you? Be honest with yourself. Every salesperson, at some point in time, has experienced a version of this scenario. In one way or another, we all have had our dealings with "call reluctance."

The biggest reason this study found for sales call reluctance was fear—fear of failure and fear of rejection. People who don't like themselves, and who don't feel confident in their abilities, are constantly held back by fear of rejection and fear of failure.

Basically, call reluctance is a fancy way of labeling underperformance. Naturally, no salesperson can be at peak performance at all times, but too many salespeople never come close to their potential. Lacking the courage to pick up the telephone and make call after call until the appointment calendar is full is one of the major factors in never realizing one's earning potential.

I can remember conducting a program for an insurance agency where there were, on the surface, many productive agents. They all had smiles, were dressed for success and were early for meetings. One morning I made a little survey to determine the extent of call reluctance within the agency. The results were astounding! Out of 19 agents, 17 scores indicated problems. Of the remaining two agents, one was fresh out of college and the other was a 12-year veteran earning in excess of $250,000 a year.

The rookie and the heavy hitter were the only people in the entire agency systematically prospecting. They were the only people contradicting the Columbia study, the only people free to reach their income potential selling insurance.

Is the fear really this damaging? Worse! New salespeople soon learn the habits dominant within the company. In the case of the insurance agency, the rookie would eventually be subjected to the "it's tough to make it in this business" attitude by everyone except the heavy hitter. Misery loves company and only the exceptional person can remain immune to such negative programming.

But the real winners in the inner sales game have a strong, positive self-image; they have confidence in their abilities and are far beyond the fear. They hit the ground running and can't wait to get to the next sales call. That's why the heavy hitters aren't around to help new salespeople, they're too busy making calls.

So a strong clue to how good you feel about yourself is how easy or hard it is for you to make sales calls.

Third, how easily do you make friends, and how well do you get along with other people? The friendship factor is a major element of selling. Customers simply won't buy from people they don't like; and likewise, you can't sell to people you don't like.

The best book on this subject is the classic *How To Win Friends And Influence People* by Dale Carnegie. I constantly recommend this book to be required reading for sales forces. If you haven't read it, do; if you haven't read it within the past three years, re-read it.

Even after digesting all the wonderful pearls Carnegie provides in his masterpiece, the fact is the better you like yourself, the easier it is to make friends and get along with people. It's that intangible quality we call personality, and it can make or break your sales career.

Fourth, how big is your circle of the possible? Can you easily see yourself becoming one of the top salespeople in the country? Can you imagine yourself becoming very successful at what you do?

Psychologists say that each of us lives within what they call a paradigm. Another name for it is a "comfort zone." It's that imaginary circle we draw around ourselves to encompass all the things we think are possible for us to do. Any time we push beyond that circle of the possible, we become frightened of the unknown.

The catch is that the size of our circle of the possible is determined by how good we feel about ourselves. The more we like ourselves, and the better we feel about our abilities, the more risk we are willing to take, the larger the circle, the greater the success we can imagine ourselves achieving. In other words we must be continually bursting out of our comfort zone to grow. We must be consistently doing things that are somewhat uncomfortable, such as prospecting, making cold calls and committing to our goals.

Most sales people have imposed very restrictive limits on themselves and what they can accomplish. They function in a negative programming cycle, full of self-limiting thoughts.

Life consists only of the world of the familiar and they dare not venture into the world of the possible. Most people are petrified of taking a chance, scared of taking a risk and failing. So they never even give themselves a chance; they don't even enter into the game. They make statements like, "I'm just not good talking to groups," so they continually pass opportunities to promote themselves and their product. Or they say, "I'm just not an organized person!", and their clutter wastes time and costs them sales. Or "I'm not good at closing!" and, guess what, few sales are closed!

The problem is, as you now know, your subconscious mind accepts those self-limiting statements as if they were fact. They become programmed habits and you act as if they are laws you dare not violate.

So, in a nutshell, the lower your self-esteem . . . the more negative your programming cycle . . . the less capable you feel. That's why it's often erroneously said that over 90 percent of our mental power goes untapped, when really it's tapped, but programmed negatively.

Steps to Correcting Low Self-Esteem

What can you do to overcome all the self-defeating, negative self-images you have programmed into your mind over the years?

To some sales trainers, the answer is always that we must start thinking positively. But I've discovered through working with thousands of people who had a very low self-concept that thinking positively over a base of negative images does not work. All that does is turn you into a St. Pollyanna, the patron saint of hopeless optimism.

Let me share with you some techniques that do work! These strategies are based on sound scientific principles and they have been tested and proven with thousands of people. They will work for you! I like to think of them as self-esteem boosters:

Self-Esteem Booster #1: The Power of Perspective. You must learn the power of perspective. Simply stated, learn to see things as they really are, not as you have imagined them to be.

Let me illustrate it like this. Just because someone has told you you'll never be successful as a salesperson does not mean you really don't have a chance to be successful. In fact, just because you've told yourself you couldn't do certain things does not mean you cannot do them.

You are a valuable, capable person, whether you ever recognize that fact or not. So why not start recognizing what is really true, that you have value as a human being, regardless of what you have led yourself to believe in the past. If you will recognize that fact, and re-program your subconscious mind to act upon that belief, you'll be amazed at how much easier your work will become and how much more successful you will be.

Let me give you another illustration of the power of perspective. If you want to be successful, you must see selling as an honorable profession. You cannot perform well in a profession you do not believe is worthy of your best efforts. But the fact is that selling is one of the oldest and most worthy professions of history.

By simply freeing yourself from any negative suggestions of others, and treating sales as a worthy profession, your subconscious mind will begin to accept this positive input about your abilities and selling, and you'll discover a whole new dimension of enthusiasm.

Self-Esteem Booster #2: The Positive Programming Cycle. Master Chapter's 12 and 13, because you must learn how to re-direct all negative self-statements. You talk to yourself constantly, whether you realize it or not. Research scientists have determined that over 85 percent of our communication is internal—to ourselves. Evidenced by the negative programming cycle, most statements to ourselves are limiting. We do it so often we forget that we are saying all those self-limiting things.

For example, maybe you had a bad time converting prospecting calls into live action—appointments—during your beginning days in the selling game. Ever since, you've been telling yourself, "I am not good at prospecting" or "I hate prospecting." Or maybe you're always making negative statements about your body.

The problem is that your subconscious mind believes all those things you say about yourself. In fact, it hears those statements as commands. For example, a few decades ago a comedienne named Totie Fields kept saying, "I've tried every diet in the world and I've concluded that the only way I'm ever going to lose weight is to lose a leg." Sure enough, she got phlebitis and lost a leg! Eventually she died from the complications. Was that just a coincidence? Maybe! But I believe, and many scientists today agree with me, that our power to control our lives by what we tell ourselves is much stronger than most of us think.

I've dedicated the past fifteen years to the study of habits, mind power and human potential. Our worst habit, the habit that holds more people back than all the others combined, is our *thinking*. Most people have developed the self-limiting habit of being in a negative programming cycle. Negative thoughts are merely repeated until they're accepted by the subconscious mind as facts, and subsequent action is a self-fulfilling prophesy.

How many prospecting calls will be made by the salesman who continually tells himself that he hates prospecting? Not many! No matter how high he sets his goals, no matter how hard he tries, not until the subconscious programming is changed will this salesman ever become a prospecting machine.

Let's look a bit further into your programming cycle. Write down all the negative self-statements you've made to yourself in the past 48 hours, and consciously re-direct them into positive self-statements. Then share this with your partner. For example:

If you said:	**Say instead:**
"I hate prospecting!"	"I love prospecting!"
"They'll never buy from me!"	"I am the best!"
"I don't like asking for referrals!"	"I always get referrals!"
"I'm afraid!"	"I'm confident!"
"I hate selling!"	"I love selling!"
"I'm not very smart!"	"I'm always learning and growing!"

By recognizing your negative self-statements and completely turning them around, you'll be amazed how your feelings about yourself will begin to change over the next few weeks. Don't concern yourself with the fact that negative thoughts enter your mind. Everybody has them. Your concern is to replace them immediately with a positive counterpart.

Self-Esteem Booster #3: Challenge All Negative Self-Beliefs. Building upon self-esteem booster #2 you're giving yourself permission to succeed by replacing all negative beliefs about yourself with positive beliefs.

This esteem booster is an action step. For example, if you believe you can't get referrals, take an existing customer or client to lunch and get three referrals. Explain that part of your income is derived from obtaining qualified referrals from good customers, that you have simply overlooked this in the past, and you'd really appreciate his or her help. You will not only get three referrals, but you'll realize how easy the process is, if you just ask. Action cures fear and boosts self-esteem.

If you feel that you're not attractive, quit telling yourself how unattractive you are and put all your energies into becoming the most attractive person you can be. Go out with someone who has good dress-for-success taste and buy the most expensive clothes you can possibly afford. This is an investment in you. The more frequently you wear nice, well-fitted clothes, the more attractive you will feel. You need to act!

What I'm saying is to quit bellyaching about all the things you don't have or can't do, and get busy doing what you can with what you have. Once you get a basic understanding of human nature you realize that people are people, very much the same!

Self-Esteem Booster #4: The Power Of Positive Visualization. You will find this to be a theme consistent throughout *Winning The Inner Game Of Selling*. I've mentioned it in previous chapters. It plays an integral role in the synergistic goal-setting exercise, and it's critical to high-level self-esteem. You must learn how to create vivid mental images of what it feels like to be a successful salesperson.

I've already talked about how to use this powerful technique. In fact, most of us already use it to some extent.

For example, we visualize how we're going to look in certain clothes, what routes we will take on the way to work. etc. Your long-range/intermediate visualization segment of synergistic goal setting is a perfect way to exercise self-esteem booster #4.

Here you are mentally rehearsing what you are going to look like when you reach your full potential. You're seeing yourself living your dreams as if they were real now. It's like creating videotapes in your mind and replaying them over and over. Every successful person you'll ever meet has been able to visualize their dream well in advance. You want to create as much sensory detail as possible in all of your visualizations.

In a moment I'm going to ask you to close your eyes, take a full breath, and visualize yourself just as you want to be, living your long-range goal, five years from now, as if it were real now. See yourself fueled with confidence, dressed for success, with all the trappings of success; be as detailed as possible. Okay, think of your dream, take a full breath and close your eyes—visualize.

Easy, isn't it? And fun!! What happens is that, as you practice your goal exercises and visualize the way you want to become, your subconscious mind begins to trigger you to act in a way that will produce that kind of results.

Athletes have used this facility of mind for centuries. If you consistently visualize yourself a tiger who can't be stopped, you'll become a tiger who can't be stopped. If you create images of yourself as a capable and confident salesperson making more and more sales, you will become just that kind of salesperson.

Summary and self-test

You're now aware that the most valuable piece of equipment you can have for winning the inner game of selling is a strong positive self-esteem. You've gotta' like yourself to be successful!

Throughout this chapter I asked a number of reflective questions to give you a feel for your own self-esteem. Now you're ready for the SEP—Self-Esteem Profile.

SEP: Self-Esteem Profile

Instructions: This inventory is designed to gauge your responses to situations involving your selling career. The objective is to assist you in becoming more aware how you really feel about yourself, without any built-in defenses.

For best results with this inventory, answer each question honestly, as you are today. This will insure maximum benefit from this profile.

After reading each statement, circle the number under the answer which best describes you.

	Strongly Agree	Mildly Agree	Mildly Disagree	Strongly Disagree
1. I am not really proud of my profession.	4	3	2	1
2. I often question my abilities to succeed in selling.	4	3	2	1
3. I think it might be easier with another product, territory, or company.	4	3	2	1
4. I tend to focus on what can go wrong, rather than what can go right.	4	3	2	1
5. I feel it's only honest to admit to a weakness.	4	3	2	1
6. I am easily intimidated by a prospect or customer.	4	3	2	1
7. Most of my efforts are focused on tasks that I am comfortable with.	4	3	2	1
8. I find myself distrustful of others.	4	3	2	1
9. I always give a sincere compliment to people when they're with me.	1	2	3	4
10. Rejection fuels my achievement drive and helps me succeed.	1	2	3	4

Scoring the SEP: You will determine your SEP score by simply adding all the numbers you have circled.

Maximum Score = 40   My Score _____

Score

10 — 14	You're self-esteem is great! Commit to the exercises in this book and you'll succeed beyond your dreams!
15 — 21	With a little attention your self-esteem will be very powerful! Make a commitment!
22 — 28	Average—let's build it up!
29 — 35	You need some real work on building your self-esteem. Master this chapter!
36 — 40	Are you in the right profession?

Areas For Improvement:

Review the individual items on the Profile and determine specific areas that you need to develop, strengthen, and enhance in your efforts to eliminate procrastination and improve performance. If you:

Circled **4**, you've identified an area to **develop.**

Circled **3**, you've identified an area to **strengthen.**

Circled **2**, you've identified an area to **enhance.**

Select *three areas* to work on between now and your next group meeting. List them below and discuss them with your partner.

#1— _____

#2— _____

#3— _____

Wrap-up

- Salespeople who feel good about themselves produce good results.
- One of the most common traits evidenced in top salespeople is a strong, positive self-image.
- Relationships impact your self-esteem; family, parents, boss, peers, clients. . . .
- Ultimately, you are responsible for your self-esteem.
- Successful salespeople are constantly expanding their world of the possible—their paradigm—comfort zone.
- Know your four self-esteem boosters!
- Be honest with yourself in the Self-Esteem Profile.

IMPORTANT STUFF!

1. List below the stuff you found important in this chapter.

_____

_____

2. What do you want to change? _____

_____

_____

3. When are you going to change it? _____

_____

_____

4. What are you going to enhance?_____

_____

_____

5. How are you going to enhance it? _____

_____

_____

Chapter 15

THE GOLDEN RULE OF SUCCESS

"I think I can, I think I can, I think I can. . . ," said the little blue engine as it strained to pull the train cars loaded with all sorts of toys for the good little boys and girls who lived on the other side of the mountain.

"I thought I could, I thought I could, I thought I could . . . ," the little blue engine said smiling as she chugged down the hill.

Many of you may remember reading "The Little Engine That Could" to your children. This classic story, as retold by Watty Piper, is full of many important messages for children and adults alike—one being the power of positive programming.

Good deeds attract success

This little train, filled with all types of presents for the children on the other side of the mountain, broke down. The toy clown and the dolls jumped out and flagged down two large engines, pleading with them to help bring these toys to the children on the other side of the mountain. But they are summarily rebuffed. These engines had no time to help a fellow engine.

Teary eyed, the clown and dolls persisted until they finally flagged down a tiny little blue engine that had never pulled a full train before, and never been over the mountain. But the little blue engine was willing to help, to do a good deed.

As the story goes, the little engine felt empathy toward the clown and dolls, and all the children on the other side of the mountain. Mustering up all the courage and strength possible by talking to herself, the little engine slowly pulled the train over the mountain.

Empowered by positive programming from repeated self-talk, elated by the accomplishment of a difficult task, the little engine gave a lesson for every salesperson to learn—the power of doing a good deed. I can remember as a Boy Scout, and later a Scoutmaster, that part of the Boy Scout oath was to do a good deed every day. This was to help you grow in character and strength. It's a universal law of nature—what goes around, comes around.

Lesson: Live By The Golden Rule

Describe your acts of good will with your working partner during your meetings. Evaluate your feelings and relate them to both your personal and professional growth. Consider the following questions for discussion:

- How does my good will to others impact me personally?

- How does my good will to others impact me professionally?

- Can I see the connection between a more helpful attitude to others and my self-esteem?

- Have I experienced anything different when talking with prospects/clients—subsequent to my involvement with a good deed?

The timelessness of the golden rule

We are living in an era of rapid change. There have been more inventions during the past ten years than in all the rest of recorded history combined. With home computers, satellite dishes, fiber optics. . . we're living in the midst of an ever-changing information age.

But what about human nature? Have we changed? Not at all! The game has changed, but human nature has remained constant. People operate in the same fashion, focused on time tested values and spiritual beliefs. Nothing can illustrate this more clearly than researching the history of The Golden Rule, which epitomizes the power of conducting good deeds.

Confucius (551-479 BC): "What you do not want done to yourself, do not do to others," from *The Chinese Classics* (1861-1886), volume 1, "The Confucian Analects," translated by James Legge. This is the first record of the golden rule.

Aristotle (384-322 BC): Confucius was followed some two hundred years later by Aristotle: "We should behave to our friends as we should wish our friends to behave to us," from *Lives Of Eminent Philosophers*, book V, section 17, by Diogenes Laertius.

Matthew 7:12: About four hundred years later, Matthew wrote "Therefore all things ye would that men should do to you, do ye so to them: for this is the law of the prophets."

Mastering the golden rule

Life is really that simple. Treat other people the way you would like to be treated, and good things will come your way. But these words go deeper than mere actions. Have you ever watched a salesperson push all the right buttons to make a sale, and, as soon as the customer was out of sight, recite a litany of negatives about the exact customer who minutes before was receiving glowing praise?

How does this make you feel? Has anybody ever treated you with such smoothness that you sensed something was missing? Salespeople of this nature are only conning themselves. The law of nature is simple; your senses are aware when the golden rule is not valued. Unfortunately, most people, not just salespeople, don't value the golden rule. This gives you a significant advantage.

You need to adhere to the totality of the golden rule and good things will come your way. There are numerous examples of this cause and effect.

Mike, a stockbroker, shared this story with me: "I always enjoyed teaching Sunday School and one Sunday afternoon I took the class to the local hospital to distribute gifts we collected to some of the needy patients. There was one elderly lady who seemed so lonely that I made a point to visit her whenever I could. After she got out of the hospital, I would help her get groceries once a week and stayed in touch.

Nine months later, she inherited close to a million dollars from an aunt who passed away. She called and asked if I would have the time to help her manage this tremendous source of money. Naturally I obliged, but in my wildest dreams I never suspected she had any money. I would never have been in that position if I wasn't doing a genuine good deed."

You can probably think of examples of your own. The point to remember is that there are no coincidences—there is no such thing as luck. But I'll bet the brokers back at the office figured Mike just got lucky with this old lady. I wonder; if they only knew...

The four parts of the golden rule

1. *Do unto others, as you would want them to do unto you.* As I mentioned in the introduction, this rule sets the tone for everything we do. Life, success and happiness is really quite simple. Sometimes the obvious is most overlooked. You will always do well by treating people as you would like to be treated.

2. *You need to think about others the way you would like them to think about you.* Good thoughts bring about good happenings. Do you think customers are going to give much repeat business to you if you're laughing behind their back? Of course not! Such negative thoughts are extremely destructive to you. They will ruin even the most positive goals.

3. *You need to empathize with people the way you would like them to empathize with you.* Salespeople who can feel for people have a much better understanding for their customers needs, can provide much more value, and sell more.

4. *You must talk to yourself the way you would like others to talk to you.* This is the least understood aspect of the golden rule, and it's really the foundation for the other three parts. You cannot think good thoughts or feelings to someone else if you don't feel good about yourself. Instead of empathizing with your customer, you feel envious. Rather than focusing on all the positive attributes of a prospect, you conduct a critical analysis—with free-flowing negative thoughts.

This is the power of positive programming. "I think I can. . ." is the little blue engine taking the golden rule full cycle. Which part comes first? It's like the old chicken and the egg question—it doesn't matter. Let's spend some time with step four.

The real power of your thoughts

You must like yourself, you must be honest with yourself, you must treat yourself as you would like others to treat you.

Helpful hint: *Trade places.* In all personal interactions, place yourself in the shoes of the other person, whether it's a purchasing agent worrying about his job if he makes another bad purchase, a flight attendant struggling with an overbooked flight, or your eight-year-old daughter who misplaced your car keys while trying to help. You will be amazed at the difference. We are naturally empathetic; it's just that we're out of practice.

186

What goes around, comes around

There are a few eternal laws of nature that have operated throughout recorded history. "As you sow, so shall you reap" is one of these laws. By determining the values (your personal mission statement) by which you guide yourself in your dealings with others, you will be fair, just and empowering. People will enjoy your company, want to conduct business with you, and treat you exactly as you've taught them, as you have treated them.

With this fundamental understanding, it's ludicrous to be unjust with others. I listen to salespeople conduct their business and so many are commiting achievement suicide. "What goes around, comes around."

Working Partner Exercise:

Share an experience with your partner of a sale in which you are not proud of your dealings. Whether the breach of trust was done by you, or your company, doesn't matter. Discuss the events of the unjust transaction: How did you feel? How much money was gained short-term? How much money was lost long-term?

As you go through these questions with your partner you become both judge and judged, student and teacher, sinner and repentor. This form of inner honesty—honesty with self—is the soul of winning the inner game. It touches every aspect of your life. Nobody can ever be perfect, but every mature human being can learn to be truthful to self and to others.

As you immerse yourself in the philosophy of the golden rule, determine to be honorable in all dealings, expect no immediate rewards. Your customers probably won't send you thank you cards for being honest. But, you will hear from a client's attorney the minute they determine any impropriety.

The rewards of honesty, of living the golden rule, are earned over time—reputation, repeat business, referrals, respect, reciprocal treatment—there can be no price tag to something so valuable.

As you really commit to the philosophy of the golden rule, you will experience a feeling of empowerment. You will know you can make a difference with every person you encounter. The simple smile, a sincere thank you, a pleasant please. . . .

Self-programming power

By understanding the basic law of the mind, it's quite simple to assess the programming power of the golden rule. You are what you think about, right? When you think good thoughts, and do good deeds, you're programming your subconscious mind for good happenings to come into your life.

As philosophers have understood for thousands of years, when you do favors for others, you receive the primary benefit. It is better to give than to receive. You will have the most significant impact on your character by adhering to this principle.

People who scheme to cheat others are unwittingly programming their subconscious mind to attract negative events into their lives. These people suffer far more than the latest victim of their deceit. How you act determines your involuntary thoughts, which ultimately determines how you feel.

When was the last time you hated a prospect, client, boss, or rival? How did this impact your performance? Understand the timeless principle of the golden rule and you know why you cannot afford to hate or envy another human being. You will learn to let go of all of the injustices that have been dumped on you, to give up on revenge, and to focus on the old saying "killing with kindness."

You fight fire with water, evil with goodness. Forget about the actions of others, this is out of your control. Concern yourself only with what you can control. The golden rule is within your control.

Wrap-up

- There are many lessons to be learned from books we read to our children—*The Little Engine That Could.*
- Commit to do a good turn everyday. What goes around, comes around . . . remember the stockbroker.
- Good turns build deep-seeded confidence.
- The golden rule is timeless: Confucius, Aristotle, and Matthew.
- Commit to the four parts of the golden rule:
    1. Do unto others as you would want them to do unto you.
    2. Think about others the way you would like them to think about you.
    3. Empathize with people, feel about people, the way you would want them to empathize (feel) about you.
    4. Talk to yourself the way you would like others to talk to you.

IMPORTANT STUFF!

1. List below the stuff you found important in this chapter.

   _____

   _____

2. What do you want to change? _____

   _____

   _____

3. When are you going to change it? _____

   _____

   _____

4. What are you going to enhance?_____

   _____

   _____

5. How are you going to enhance it? _____

   _____

   _____

Chapter 16

JUST DO IT!

By nature, men are all alike, but their habits carry them
far apart.   —Confucius

We've covered a lot of ground in a short period of time. But, much
like any classroom learning nothing is significant until somebody starts
doing. Take the previous chapter as a perfect example. Everyone knows
they should treat others as they desire to be treated. The golden rule
is some 4,000 years old! But knowing and doing are often miles apart!
You are going to be a confirmed doer!

I've listened to salespeople who spoke so eloquently about their product . . . market conditions . . . sales strategies that complement the market . . . their integrity . . . but, they never were able to sell much. And,
often in desperation, they would stretch the truth to get a sale. If you
were to ask them about their application of the golden rule they might
score themselves highly. But, if they were doing all the exercises and
working with a partner, they couldn't get away with such behavior.

An old saying that most everyone has heard sums this up very well,
"Your actions speak so loudly, I can't hear what you say." Too many
salespeople fall into this trap. They talk instead of "act." Your challenge is to act upon the message in this book. Initially you might be
forced to act when you don't quite believe in yourself. That's okay.
The objective of winning the inner game of selling is to help you ger-
minate this belief. This requires action.

Think of the high achievers you know. Do they believe in themselves? You bet! Did they always? I'm sure many started their success journey, just like you, searching for answers, but full of skepticism and doubt. Yet, they acted. They learned how to believe in themselves, their profession, and developed the habit of *doing*. This is the essence of "million dollar success habits."

As Professor William James, the noted father of behavioral psychology in America, said "The great thing in all education is to make our nervous system our ally instead of our enemy. For this we must make automatic and habitual, as early as possible, as many useful actions as we can." Continuing, this great Harvard professor said, "Seize the very first possible opportunity to act on every resolution, and on every emotional prompting you may experience in the direction of the habits you aspire to gain." How are you doing? Have you seized the first opportunity to act on these inner game tactics?

What have you done?

You've already completed 15 chapters of this book and are in the final stretch of ingesting all of these wonderful pearls of wisdom. But they're all meaningless if not acted upon. I would be remiss if I didn't hold you accountable for doing what you're learning.

I'm going to be easy on you, but my point will be firm. With your working partner, list five DO'S that have been completed from the chapters you've read. Next, list five TO-DO'S that will be attended to within 24 hours. For example, working through the golden rule application exercise in Chapter 15 is a DO, putting it off is procrastination!

My Five DO's
1. _____
2. _____
3. _____
4. _____
5. _____

Working Partner's Five DO'S
1. _____
2. _____
3. _____
4. _____
5. _____

My Five TO-DO's
1. _____
2. _____
3. _____
4. _____
5. _____

Working Partner's TO-DO's
1. _____
2. _____
3. _____
4. _____
5. _____

You should use this exercise every time you adjust your goals. Quantum leaps in production, in personal growth, must be definitively broken down into their lowest component parts. These are the simple DO'S that initiate all those wonderful results.

The control cycle of habits

Dick, a recent attendee at one of my seminars, recalled how his nervous system transformed from ally to enemy, "It used to be that I couldn't wait to go to work every morning! I was on the phone all day writing business. I was proud of myself. And then something happened. . ." and after a thoughtful pause, he continued, "I seem to have lost my spark. I don't think it was any one thing, but I'm not sure how I feel about the business, and I don't feel like prospecting."

How do you feel about prospecting?

Regardless of what you sell, can you relate to Dick? When was the last time you didn't feel like making those prospecting calls? Or, better yet, how do you feel about making prospecting calls right now? I know that's not fair; you're working on your career as you work through this book. But my message remains: How often does your prospecting activity become negatively impacted because of how you feel?

What about your thoughts?

At times, do your thoughts echo Dick's? Does the thought of prospecting excite you? Do you like working the phone, meeting new people and presenting yourself? Do you get fired-up making calls? What are your thoughts about getting referrals? Even as you strive to unlock your potential as a professional salesperson, you still might not think you can pull it off. Right? I know many salespeople, when asked, dislike all the activities mentioned above, yet are quite successful. Why? Because they act! They do these necessary activities, even when they don't like them. Are you willing? Consider every exercise in this book, each action step, your working partnership . . . they are all acts.

What are you doing now?

I want to restate the simple achievement cycle formula which can be applied to all facets of winning the inner game. For clarification of terms, activity is doing. You can control your thinking, and how you feel, by what you do—*action*. Let's take another look at the basics of what makes us function. Consider this cycle:

This is the foundation for all habits as every repetition of an act makes you more likely to perform that act, and discover the wonderful natural law—the Law of Control. Let's revisit each component individually, the relationship with the cycle, and your productivity.

1. *Doing:* Walking, talking, reading this book, meeting with your partner, phoning, asking for referrals, are acts—do's—which involve the controlled, voluntary movement of some part of the body. You are in complete control over this component. This is the action phase of the cycle, and because of this, it dictates the remaining components. As I've said before: *Action* cures fear, *action* builds confidence, *action* gets results.

To acquire million dollar success habits, to win the inner game of selling, you must begin this cycle with a DO! You need to act upon something you might not think favorably about—making cold prospecting calls, asking existing clients for referrals, prospecting friends, meeting with your working partner and being held accountable.

Of equal importance, you must act in a manner that you might not feel good about. The DO might be creating tension, such as committing to specific goals that will require a quantum leap. Nevertheless you have to work through the tension.

For example: Let's say your thoughts about doubling your income are "I don't think I'm capable. I just know I'm going to fail." And your feelings that are driving these thoughts range from nervousness to outright fear—the typical reaction resembles paralysis. There's no activity! You do nothing and, therefore, effectively make your thoughts and feelings a self-fulfilling prophecy. In this scenario, you're working the cycle backwards.

The average person makes this critical error of allowing their feelings to dictate their thoughts, which impact their actions, or more accurately, inaction. This is why so many people, not just salespeople, never come close to realizing their potential. In the sales game, salespeople simply retire, but don't quit. Do you know anybody like this? They come to work everyday, make all indication of working, but don't call, procrastinate, etc. Label it call reluctance, laziness, whatever, many different forms of career threatening behaviors are created from not understanding the law of control. Why? Because they never repeat an act.

But what if you could act in just the opposite manner? Okay, you're buying into winning the inner game of selling, but you've yet to establish a working partner—you're afraid to be put down, you don't think anybody wants to work towards maximizing their potential, but *you ask!* This is doing, an act. And you ask a fellow salesperson. What's going to happen? Well, if they agree, you're off and running. If they have to think about it, ask someone else.

Sometimes getting started requires more work. Not only will you be fighting negative thoughts and feelings, you'll have to develop an organized approach to developing these million dollar success habits. But you are acting!

Somewhere during the second week, as you maintain your doing, you will start to impact your thinking. Maybe you've made a big sale, had an excellent working partner meeting, received good feedback, helped your partner start to believe, and you begin to think, "Hey, I can really achieve the success I've always dreamed about." Shortly, following this change in thinking, you'll start to influence how you feel about yourself and all the necessary DO'S in your business. The fear you used to experience is being replaced with excitement and anticipation.

2. *Thinking:* I've discussed this in depth in earlier chapters, but suffice it to say, we all have voluntary and involuntary thoughts. As you know, most people have developed the self-limiting habit of thinking in a negative programming cycle. They dwell on negatives until they become worries. And worry is a form of mental cancer! Since most of you reading this book are already caught up in this self-limiting cycle, the most expedient recourse is *doing.*

But here's the catch; the path of least resistance for any person trapped in this negative cycle is to act in accordance to their programming. In other words, to do nothing. Acting in a productive fashion involves stepping out of the comfort zone. For many, reading these pages is out of the comfort zone. This can be a scary feeling, but stay with it.

What's an appropriate DO? Recording your most powerful self-help tape. Have you? Many people put this off. Don't! Who cares if you're not certain about your statements, or whether you need to buy a recorder that records. DO! You can always change your affirmations and re-record.

3. *Feeling:* We have a wide range of feelings. They're as much a part of our total behavior as doing and thinking; anger, joy, fear, excitement, motivation, laziness, and on they go. Most salespeople, like most people, act in relation to their feelings. If it feels good, they do it. Or, how often have you heard yourself, or another salesperson in your office say, "I just didn't feel like doing anything today."?

People are feeling driven because it is the path of least resistance. Living in a world of the familiar, they remain deep inside their comfort zones. Many salespeople I've worked with have been aware of this malaise, but didn't have a clue to how to change.

Jim, a North Carolina insurance salesman, who attended a million dollar success habit seminar that I conducted, summed up his dilemma. "I don't feel comfortable asking for referrals, so I never ask. I don't feel comfortable calling on neighbors and friends, so I have none for clients. Yet . . . ." And then in an apologetic tone he concluded, "My manager tells me I have the potential to be one of the top producers of our agency." What do you think of Jim's potential?

Like so many, Jim is full of options; he doesn't have to venture out of his comfort zone. He has the option to hang in there trying to sell insurance, find another job, supplement his income, or even collect welfare. But if Jim was confronted with an uncomfortable situation with no options, such as a fire in his office, he would act. He would call the fire department, grab the fire extinguishers, possibly even become a hero. He would act outside of his comfort zone, free of consultation with his dominating thoughts and feelings. Ah, but with the fire, there were no options! Right?!

What are your options? Do you have any alternatives? Or is there a fire brewing, even as you read through this book, that's threatening to turn your career into ashes? I keep reading of experts citing figures of salespeople who flush out of selling every year. Is this really an option? Not on your life! You're winning the inner game!

What are your options?

The more you apply the achievement cycle of Doing-Thinking-Feeling to the contents of this book, the more control you will have over everything in your life. There is nothing magical here, rather a basic law of human nature. Let me give you a simple exercise to demonstrate:

Feelings: As you read these words, try to feel fear. Conjure up all those gut-wrenching feelings you might associate with prospecting, cold calling, whatever. Try to feel fear. Can you do it? It's not easy, is it? In fact it's just about impossible, because nothing is happening to generate those feelings.

Thinking: Now try to think about your biggest client. Get the image of this person in your mind as clearly as you can. This you can do, but it requires concentration. As soon as your mind relaxes, thoughts of this client slip away.

Doing: Now take your left hand and touch your left ear. Just do it. Easy, isn't it. Or, pick up the phone and dial the operator. Without any hesitation, you can touch your left ear with your left hand, you can dial that number.

What's important to realize, *doing* is under your complete control. You might think "It's stupid for me to touch my ear", but you still can touch it easily. You might not feel any reason to call the operator, but you can still easily, DO.

You might think it's useless to make all those calls. Maybe you feel awkward calling. This doesn't matter, you can still DO! You must DO! But you must have a game plan for your DO'S. I've yet to see salespeople enjoy any long-term benefits, any true behavioral change, by putting off the action steps I was teaching. Don't *think* about making your self-programming tape, *make* it!

If you want to be an average salesperson, let your feelings drive you as you work through this book. Stay comfortable, think about these exercises rather than act upon them, and you might end up with a terminal case of procrastination. Nobody's impervious! If you want to be a high achiever, ACT NOW! Commit to mastering the inner game of selling! Break out of your comfort zone and DO! Activity drives the dream, controls the thoughts, fuels your feelings, and gets results!

JUST DO IT!

Wrap-up

- "Your actions speak so loudly, I can't hear what you're saying."
- List your five DO's.
- List your five TO-DO's.
- The achievement cycle, doing-thinking-feeling, is the foundation of all habits.
- Most people are feeling driven—they do what feels comfortable.
- Successful salespeople DO!
- Let your actions, DO's, create tension as this stimulates growth.

IMPORTANT STUFF!

1. List below the stuff you found important in this chapter.

_____

_____

2. What do you want to change? _____

_____

_____

3. When are you going to change it? _____

_____

_____

4. What are you going to enhance?_____

_____

_____

5. How are you going to enhance it? _____

_____

_____

Chapter 17

ENLIGHTENMENT

I hear and I forget. I see and I remember. I experience and
I understand. —Chinese proverb

There are many ways to describe enlightenment. I've chosen to paraphrase the story of three cats as told by Taisen Deshimaru in his book, *The Zen Way to the Martial Arts*. As you read through this fascinating tale, make note of yourself, your working partner, and any other sales person who fits the description of a particular cat. Write these lessons in the space provided, along with any other thoughts, comments etc. Then have a discussion. Actually there are five cats to discuss.

"Two hundred years or so ago in Japan, there was a samurai warrior whose home was infested by a huge rat. Every night this big rat came to the samurai's house and kept him awake. Annoyed, he consulted a Zen monk at a nearby temple who trained cats. The samurai said, 'Lend me your best cat.'

"The Zen monk lent him an alley cat, extremely quick and adept at rat catching, with stout claws and far-springing muscles. But when he came face to face with the rat in the room, the rat stood his ground and the cat ran. There was something very special about that rat.

"The samurai then borrowed a second cat, a ginger one, with terrific energy and an aggressive personality. This second cat stood his ground, fought with the rat, but the rat got the best of it and the cat beat a hasty retreat.

"A third cat was procured and pitted against the rat—this one was black and white—but could do no better than the other two.

"The samurai then borrowed yet another cat, the fourth; it was black and old and not stupid, but not so strong as the alley cat or the ginger cat. It walked into the room. The rat stared at it awhile, then moved forward. The black cat sat down, very collected, and remained utterly motionless. A tiny doubt flitted through the rat. He edged a little closer; he was just a little bit afraid. Suddenly the cat caught him by the neck and killed him.

"Then the samurai warrior went to the monk and said to him 'How many times have I chased that rat with my wooden sword, but instead of hitting him he would scratch me; why was your black cat able to get him?'

"The monk suggested he call a meeting and ask the cats themselves. So there was an assembly of cats, presided over by the black cat which was the oldest. The alley cat took the floor and said, 'I am very strong.' The black cat answered, 'Then why didn't you win?'

"The alley cat answered, 'Really, I am very strong; I know hundreds of different techniques for catching rats. But this was no ordinary rat.'

"The black cat said, 'So your strength and your techniques aren't equal to those of the rat. Maybe you have lots of muscles, but skill alone was not enough.' "

LESSON:

- Who does the alley cat remind you of?
- What sales lessons are presented by this cat?

"Then the ginger cat spoke: 'I am enormously strong, I exercise, eat healthy foods, and have tremendous energy. But I too was unable to overcome the rat. Why?'

"The old black cat answered, 'Your activity and energy are great indeed, but the rat was beyond your energy; you are weaker than that big rat because you are attached to your ego, proud of it, and it interferes with your energy. You are weak because you have too much confidence in yourself.' "

LESSON:

- Who does the ginger cat remind you of?
- What sales lesson is presented by this cat?

Next came the black and white cat, which had also been defeated. He wasn't as strong as the others, but he was intelligent and spent all his time practicing techniques—but because he never had a goal or desire for profit, he too had to run for his life.

LESSON:

- Who does the black and white cat remind you of?
- What sales lesson is presented by this cat?

"The black cat told him, 'You are extremely intelligent, and strong, too. But you couldn't beat the rat because you lacked goal focus, so the rat's intuition was more effective than yours. The instant you walked into the room it understood your attitude and state of mind, and that's why you could not overcome it. You were unable to harmonize your strength, your technique, and your creative consciousness; they remained separate instead of blending into one.

" 'Whereas I, in a single moment, used all three faculties unconsciously, naturally and automatically, and that is how I was able to kill the rat.' "

LESSON:

- Who does the black cat remind you of?
- What sales lessons are presented by the black cat?

" 'But I know a cat, in a village not far from here, that is even stronger than I am, yet there is nothing strong-looking about him. He is very, very old, his whiskers are gray, and he sleeps all day. He has never caught a single rat because they're all scared to death of him. He could chase them in his sleep. You must become like him; beyond posture, beyond breathing, beyond consciousness.' "

LESSON:

- Who does the very, very old cat remind you of?
- What sales lessons were presented by the very old cat?

If you're still wondering where I've taken you with this cat story, relax you ginger cat, you have just begun a remarkable journey! All the exercises I've described in previous chapters involve self-awareness, re-programing, and strategic action. The purpose is to take you through the various stages of growth illustrated by these cats, with your ultimate destination somewhat similar to the very old cat.

You've only just begun!

Wouldn't it be nice to have earned such a reputation as a salesperson that when anyone thinks of a need in your field they call you? This has happened, but only after years of enlightened living, selling, and personal growth. It's essential to understand, by experiencing this message, that you've only just begun. You're setting standards for yourself, your working partner and your family, that transcend societal norms.

As an achievement-focused sales person, your life is going to be one continuous series of experiences that take you outside of your comfort zone—expanding you as a person, and your world of the possible. Yes, your life is truly a journey! The only constant will be *change.*

By welcoming the challenges that accompany winning the inner game of selling, you've acknowledged personal responsibility for growth through change, and accepted personal control over this very special journey. The following questions are to be answered with your working partner and discussed relative to how you perceive yourself now, not when you began this book. Some of these questions might have been asked earlier, that's okay, the object is your *enlightenment* now.

Working Partner Exercise:

1. What is the meaning of your life? _____

_____

2. What is there about your career as a professional salesperson that gives your life additional purpose and meaning? _____

_____

3. How are you nurturing the balance in your life (family, spiritual and professional)? _____

_____

4. What are your current thoughts about other living creatures, the environment, the planet earth? _____

_____

5. Do you feel tapped in to a higher power? If so, what is your relationship with that higher power? _____

_____

This is not an easy working partner exercise. Then, of course, nothing of value ever is. I'm asking you to go deep inside yourself, searching for answers much in the manner a musician searches for that perfect sound. After completing your search, you must expose yourself by sharing your answers with your working partner. I'm asking you to rethink, like a musician tunes sounds of magic into an instrument. This is the essence of winning the inner game of selling.

More sales will come naturally as you take residence on a higher plane of consciousness. You won't have a lot of company at this address and you won't always feel comfortable here. But, you will be committed to a higher standard . . . you'll be constantly tuning your magic . . . and you will DO to the best of your ability.

This is enlightenment. As one becomes enlightened, whether through this book or other means, it leads to spirituality. It's been said that over 99 percent of the people in the western world live on a lower level of consciousness, characterized by an unquenchable thirst for security, sex, ego satisfaction, prestige, power, money and status. The result is a frustrating journey filled with fear, worry, resentment and anger. Every accomplishment brings more frustration than joy because of this unquenchable thirst.

You are prepared for ongoing growth, high level achievement, and natural happiness. As you focus your energies inward, you control your response to life, rather than futilely trying to control life itself. The more thoroughly we know ourselves, our strengths and weaknesses, the more aware we become of what is within our control. This is freedom in the true sense, from the inside-out.

Your Spiritual Power

Enlightenment personifies personal awareness, allowing for visions and understanding free of ego interference (remember the lessons of the ginger cat). The magic within you, the internal power I've been discussing and demonstrating with exercises throughout these chapters, is in many ways your source of spirituality.

When, through your experiences, you thoroughly understand the inner game, you become at peace with yourself, your career, and the world around you. In Alcoholics Anonymous, this spirituality is referred to as the "higher power" or God, as your religious beliefs interpret God. Yes, I firmly believe there is a higher power and in my life, with my family, we call this power God.

Enlightenment is freedom, but it carries an awesome responsibility. I believe there is no one "right" way to believe in God, as long as you accept your freedom and the accompanying responsibility. This requires a personal relationship with your higher power.

What I'm referring to transcends organized religion, although many serve this purpose very well. The enlightened respect the beliefs of others. They aren't intimidated by a difference of opinion, they are no longer threatened by someone different—as long as that person is *good!*

Do you know any enlightened people? How tolerant are you of the beliefs of others? Do you know anyone who always is trying to convert, avoid or challenge people who are different? Are these people at peace inside? I doubt it! Are they positioned for high achievement? No!

The God I believe in accepts all forms of belief in a higher power. My God is more concerned with how frequently you apply the golden rule, rather than where you worship, what books you read, and how fluently you can recite verse, prayers, etc. The higher power in my life is very forgiving, but is constantly challenging us to grow. This is why adversity, struggles and failure have been experienced by most high achievers.

A book that I highly recommend is Viktor Frankl's, *Man's Search For Meaning,* as Dr. Frankl writes of the horrors he experienced when incarcerated by the Nazis in Auschwitz. Written from the clinical viewpoint of a psychiatrist, which he was, Dr. Frankl shares his insights into human behavior, spirituality, suffering, and will have you rethinking your "meaning" in life.

The journey

Always keep your eyes focused toward the future, not the past. As the great baseball pitcher Satchel Page once said, "Don't look back, someone might be gaining on you." Nobody's journey is without suffering, embarrassment and failure; if it is, they aren't on a journey—these people are merely existing.

Many people are familiar with Abraham Lincoln's difficult route to the White House. It was anything but free from suffering, embarrassment and failure. But it was loaded with belief. Let's take a brief look:

- Failed in business in 1831;
- Defeated for Legislature in 1832;
- Second failure in business in 1833;
- Nervous breakdown in 1836;
- Defeated for Speaker in 1838;
- Defeated for Elector in 1840;
- Defeated for Congress in 1843;
- Defeated for Congress in 1848;
- Defeated for Senate in 1855;
- Defeated for Vice President in 1856;
- Defeated for Senate in 1858;
- Elected President in 1860.

Lincoln was always growing, learning, dreaming and struggling. As far as formal religion was concerned, it wasn't until he was torn apart inside, over the carnage of the Civil War, that he began regular attendance in church. Yet Abraham Lincoln was always known as man full of goodness.

I pray that none of us will ever be tested as severely as Abraham Lincoln or Victor Frankl. But then we must be more dedicated to our enlightenment. Each of us has much to give. You have an obligation to nurture your talent, reach for your potential, and then share your lessons with others.

Ego interference

Enlightenment puts you on track to: first, do what is right inside you, then apply those principles to the outside world, and finally, be free from being judgmental of others. This is a far cry from those people who are self-righteous, full of piety . . . and blame. They are burdened by ego interference; again, the ginger cat. To maximize your potential as a sales person and a human being, you must leave judgment and blame behind.

This is one of those things that is simple, but not easy. True enlightenment is simple. As you grow with your working partner you can gauge enlightenment by the following criteria; Are you or your working partner blaming or judgmental? If you are, your responsibility is to address this issue, as a team. Whenever you hear blame or judgment, ego interference is occurring. If left unchecked it can lead to at best, harmless bad judgment, and at worst, life threatening behavior.

Covering up insecurities by casting blame on others never works. Recognize your insecurities . . . accept responsibility for them . . . act in a manner that can help diffuse them, and practice that action to keep them far away. This is enlightenment. As it's been written, God helps those who help themselves—not those who blame others.

Use your higher power, help yourself, and make a commitment to helping others. We all share the responsibility to live by the golden rule and make the world a better place. By winning the inner game of selling you will significantly increase your income, but you'll also be playing an important role in changing the perception of salespeople. Through your actions—your commitment, your personal growth—you will make it easier for others to follow in your footsteps. Continue forward with an enlightened heart, an open mind, and goal-focused discipline.

And as you step into your journey every day—going for it—think of this poem by Joseph Norris:

> Drop a pebble in the water,
>   And its ripples reach out far;
> And the sunbeams dancing on them
>   May reflect them to a star.
> Give a smile to someone passing,
>   Thereby making his morning glad;
> It may greet you in the evening
>   When your own heart may be sad.
> Do a deed of simple kindness;
>   Though its end you may not see.
> It may reach, like widening ripples,
>   Down a long eternity.

Wrap-up

- Enjoy your journey.
- Keep up with your working partner.
- Don't look for perfection; rather insist upon consistency of action, congruent values, and far-reaching goals.
- Oh yes, always remember to teach the principles of winning the inner game of selling to others, and may God bless your wondrous journey!

IMPORTANT STUFF!

1. List below the stuff you found important in this chapter.

_____

_____

2. What do you want to change? _____

_____

_____

3. When are you going to change it? _____

_____

_____

4. What are you going to enhance?_____

_____

_____

5. How are you going to enhance it? _____

_____

_____

PRODUCTS AVAILABLE

• WINNING THE INNER GAME OF SELLING

Research has shown that up to 90% of performance in selling comes from the "inner game". Self confidence and the ability to overcome fear, will allow you to reach your earning potential. Let Matt teach you step, by step, how to win the "inner game" and increase your earnings.

(book and 6 cassettes)	**$75.00**
Book only	**$18.00**
Tapes only	**$65.00**

• THE NEW PSYCHOLOGY OF SELLING

Learn how to understand your customer and their anxieties. You will learn how to become a consultive sales person, helping people make buying decisions by solving problems. Turn tension into sales, develop responsive strategies that increase your selling power. This series offers you dynamic and power packed sales success strategies **$65.00**

• THE AUTOHYPNOSIS DIET

Matt shows you how to look better and feel better and most importantly how to stay that way. You'll need no more fad diets. Now you'll have a positive means to control your weight for a lifetime. (6 cassettes) **$59.95**

• ReEVALUATING YOUR LIFE

Fine-tune your life with these Life Steps: Where are you now? - What's important to you? - Who are you? - Capitalizing on your strengths. - An Achievement Mindset - Goal Getting - Role Model Power - Your Master Plan - Creating a support group. - Perpetual Growth.

Six Audiocassetes plus Interactive Workbook **$59.95**

• STRENGTHS/WEAKNESS ASSESSMENT

A unique cognitive instrument that measures an individual's perception, awareness, capacities and capabilities within the world of selling/mgnt. Nine broad areas and 68 specific areas are measured. Major areas include prospecting, probing, meeting prospects, closing, motivators, empathy, achievement drive, commitment to selling/mgnt. and stress factors. 9-13 page analysis

Sales	**$65.00**
Management	**$65.00**

• THE BEHAVORIAL/PERSONALITY ANALYSIS

Provides details on an individual's style of selling, overcoming objections, closing and servicing accounts. Learn how to spot winners in management or sales and establish a reliable method of choosing salespeople. Can also be used to evaluate the performance of both new and existing employees or self evaluation. (Can be adapted to sales or mangement focus.) **$50.00**

TO ORDER VIA MASTERCARD OR VISA CALL: 800-883-6582 or COMPLETE COUPON ON NEXT PAGE AND ENCLOSE CHECK

For more information call us at 910-273-6582

ORDER FORM

Company Name _____

Attention _____

Shipping Address _____

City, State & Zip _____

Telephone Day _____ **Night** _____

ITEM DESCRIPTION	PRICE	QUANTITY	TOTAL COST

Make Checks Payable To: The Oechsli Institute

Total Order _____

☐ Check

☐ Visa   ☐ MasterCard   Shipping* _____

Exp. Date _____

Card Number _____   Total Due _____

Signature _____

* Shipping charges $3.00 per first item.
  $1.50 for each additional item.

Mail to: The Oechsli Institute, P.O. Box 29385, Greensboro, NC 27429
Fax to: 910-273-2342 or Call us at 910-273-6582